Y0-CPB-061

THE GIFTED & THE WORTHLESS

Observations of a Guest Teacher

Matthew Lotti

ISBN: 9781795775212

© Copyright 2019 Matthew Lotti. All rights reserved.

For the resilient.

"This civilization is on fire; the whole thing is capsizing and sinking. What splendid torpedoing!"

Guy Debord,
In girum imus nocte et consumimur igni

1. An Introduction.

It could have been a Wednesday. It could have been a Thursday. The days, by that point, were quite a jumble. But there I was: scrambling around a small, disheveled room, floor littered with green building blocks and fragments of crayon, disoriented and jittery from too much coffee due to too little sleep. I was struggling, *in vain*, to remove from the dirty palms of about twenty kindergarten children the plastic rulers they were using to *smack* each other in the face. The plastic rulers had their names on them, so it wasn't like they *weren't* supposed to have them, but the rulers weren't given to be weapons. And these critters: they're a quick bunch, tiny and elusive, darting around the room like Barry Sanders in his prime. Afterwards, when I finally got rid of the pests, and watched as they boarded their noon buses to return to their homes, I rubbed my temples with the tips of my fingers, wondering *what am I doing here*? This is what alcohol was invented for. Teachers.

I clearly recall, as an Elementary School student, that I never had the faintest desire to grow up and become a teacher. If you asked a 12-year-old me what dream job I'd love to have, I would have probably told you I wanted to be James Bond (I was hooked on movies from an early age; most kids were busy watching cartoons on Saturday morning while I was idolizing Sean Connery and re-watching *Thunderball*) or maybe a fighter pilot, but never a teacher. When I was in High School I did not want to be a teacher. I wanted to be a filmmaker, reading books on Martin Scorsese and Oliver Stone and David Lynch during study hall. When I was in college, I did not want to be a teacher, and kept an eye on the Wild World of Finance. That's why I never majored in Elementary or Secondary Education. But as it turned out, for several years following my tragic graduation day, that would be what I would wake up and do during the week. I had no training, no background, no inkling as to what to do, but there I was, staring at dirty faces and gap-toothed grins and T-shirts with cartoon characters on them, armed with a cup of coffee in one hand and the barest of lesson plans in the other. I can't tell you which Circle of Hell I was in, but I can tell you it was one of the deep ones, and if I had ever wronged anyone so badly as to warrant that kind of bad karma, please line up and I will apologize on both knees.

The decision to become a teacher was not immediate. I dabbled here and there, but nothing fit me. I couldn't stand cubicle work, so that was immediately out of the question - a month-long stint at some soul-killing factory was enough for me. I was so bored with the job I would routinely leave my desk and wander around the building, engaging in oddball games like collecting pens or skipping around all four floors just to kill time. My co-slaves wouldn't stand for it, my boss wouldn't stand for it, and they treated me like a child, even creating for me a "Sign Out" book, so that even when I had to go to the bathroom, I was timed (it's strange how life works, because this would be apt foreshadowing for my 'next' profession). After leaving that 8-to-5 debacle, several people did their part in offering suggestions as to different places I could send my resume or different career paths I could take, but they never panned out - at most, after four years of faxing or mailing cover sheets and work references, I only had *two* interviews. Not wanting to work in retail, I resigned myself to part-time instructional duties.

The 'process' of becoming a teacher is disgustingly simple, at least for the school district I was at, referred to hereafter as the "District." If you have a college degree in, well, anything, you can get an Emergency Certificate from the state. This grants you permission to substitute in any building in the District, although some full-time teachers who were snuck in by the administration or 'people they know' actually have Emergency Certificates and are sliding by on technicalities (for example, one gentleman I spoke with was an engineer, retired, and spoke fluent German, and since they couldn't seem to find any German teachers, he was given the job). You need to have two important checks done by the state: the Child Abuse Clearance and the Criminal Check. Get the two Checks and the Emergency Certificate, drop them off with an application at the Human Resources office, check off which grades (K-5? 6-8? 9-12? All of them??) you want to teach on your application folder and that's it. You wait for the phone call from the Substitute Caller.

I'm sure you might be thinking that there are intermediary steps involved. Certainly not. You need to get two or three interviews to work at a local grocery store and at least two to work at a certain bookstore chain, but none are needed to be a substitute teacher. Also, no classes are given to tell you how to conduct a class, how to discipline students, what can be said and what cannot be said. I always felt as if it were never a concern whether or not I knew how to conduct a class. Was I a living body? Did I have no sense of self-esteem? Did I not mind being verbally abused and ignored? Come on in, sit down, and teach these kids algebra! We've been waiting for you!

The schools, at least in our District, were never the ones to call for substitutes. They had two separate people doing that work: the Elementary Caller (in charge of the 15 grade schools) and the Middle & High School Caller (who covered all four Middle Schools and the two High Schools). The Middle & High School Caller, a malevolent, senile old woman who I'll refer to as Batty, had been doing it for over a decade before retiring recently - she was given to yelling at people she called for not wanting certain undesirable classes like Special Ed. or Physical Education; you should be simply honored she picked up the phone to breathe into your ear - and the Elementary Caller ... who, well, is not one person, but *several* people. Truth is, they must have gone through countless Elementary Substitute callers during the last couple of years, and no one that gets the job keeps it for long. I had gotten to know one of them very well before she left the job - she threw her books (literally) at the Director of Human Resources (also known as Herr Director) - sick of the misguided whims of the Principals and their equally dopey Secretaries, who couldn't figure out what teachers were out and which were in. This doesn't sound like a complicated task, but most of these females only went to High School and struggled to figure out how to operate a laminating machine or replace a toner cartridge in the fax machine. I can't tell you how many times I had to wander down the hallways trying to find other teachers to see which one of their own was out. Few ever seemed to know what the hell was going on ("Oh, Kim's out today? I didn't know that" was one generic, dazed response).

Getting calls from the Substitute Callers were infrequent but I didn't mind, because I privately never wanted to get called. I worked some smaller jobs during my teaching days, one of which was doing janitorial work, and I found that much more rewarding. I would show up at the office after hours (7 PM-ish), clean the bathrooms, vacuum the carpets and mop the floors and be out of there without interference. (It's degrading but simple, and sometimes you just want a little peace and quiet.)

Life without interference was rare when teaching. I was usually walking on proverbial eggshells waiting for someone to accuse me of something. If I got through the day and no one accosted me, and if one of the Substitute

Callers didn't ring my house telling me there was a complaint with the way I handled something and none of the teachers or Principals questioned me on some statement a student accused me of uttering, it was a great relief.

Why bother at all you ask? Frankly, the pay was a big perk. At $90 a day, it paid better - and had better hours - than most any part-time job I could think of that didn't involve computer programming. Grade schools ran from 8:15 to 3:30, Middle Schools from 8:15 to 3:00 and High Schools from 7:30 to 2:30. But most of the time at the end of the day I would almost drift off and slog myself home, feeling physically drained from trying to keep control on classrooms filled with anywhere from 15 to 25 kids who thought, hooray, we have a substitute in for Mr./Ms./Mrs. Whoever, *it's a free day for us, let's make this difficult on him.* And a lot of the time they did. And what a drag that was.

In a perverse way, one of the 'benefits' of the job was my ability to actually use my Psychology degree, since there's no better battlefield with which to test the things I learned in college. Several people I confided to - privately - that I had no desire to teach, that I was just doing this for the money, told me that if anything, Psychology should be just as helpful in dealing with the young as a degree in Elementary Education. Which is true, I think, but it's harder for me, personally, to work Psychological Miracles on a larger group than it is on a smaller group, or perhaps on a one-to-one level. If I was trying to settle down someone in one corner of the room, on the other side of the room there was something that was happening. And when I turned around, two kids would be standing there, one wanting to make a phone call to his Mom, another wanting to go to the nurse for something akin to a paper cut (toughen up, Marine, I wanted to say), and maybe two or three raised hands among the school desks all needing a variety of things. My head would often not know where to turn to next and I would find myself repeating things over and over again. For comic effect, one day when I lost my voice, I made up paper signs that said, "Sit down!" and "Stop talking!" and "Yes, you can go to the bathroom." The novelty of this lasted just long enough to get me through the day and home to some tea with honey, but strangely enough, those were the only three directives I needed to have written down.

It is my goal, with this book, to convey in some way what happens when parents send their kids off to class and touch upon the disillusionment that's evident in some of the full-time teachers I've met. Do you know your children lie? A lot? Do you have any clue about the barbarism that takes place in the Middle and High Schools? Do you think children are being left behind? Do you have any idea how burned out some of these teachers really are, how lapse the school board can be or how hostile Principals can be? I've spent several years of my life exposed to the seemingly random chaos that takes place, and some of it is so outlandish you may not believe it yourself. Is it sensational? Absolutely, but it's all true. God help us.

2. The Problem with Principals.

It did not take me long to discover that the Principals of these schools - having acquired their jobs through years of sweat and labor or perhaps an advanced form of sorcery - are some of the biggest divas around, and require constant monitoring on the part of the substitute. I also discovered that they are not the kind of people with whom you want to make small talk. I didn't realize this in the beginning, and found myself faced with several problems - it wasn't until I learned to duck and evade that I found my life easier.

In their defense, being a Principal is not an easy job. Oh, sure, they make well over $100k a year (according to the records, which are public domain), but it is stressful. Teachers complain to them about their students, parents complain to them about their teachers they're in charge of - and ultimately responsible for - every fiasco that comes along. I can only imagine it's like being the General of an Army. And just like Generals in the Army, this 'leadership role' can lead to paranoia and power trips. Being but a junior cadet with sweat still fresh on my brow, well, this made me the target of suspicious glances and 'drop-ins,' wherein they 'observe' how I'm handling the class, no training (on my part) at all.

While I've heard horror stories about at least 2/3 of the Principals in the District, I only had major issues with two, minor issues with another six or so and heard stories about most of the rest. I think it has to do with personalities, and mine clashed with two of them in a big way. In order to conceal their identities, I'm going to refer to them as Mrs. Tweedle-Dum and Mrs. Tweedle-Dee. Being likeminded and of a similar disposition, they tried putting their heads together to get me fired during my first year. It didn't work, obviously, but it put a scare into me.

Mrs. Tweedle-Dum and Mrs. Tweedle-Dee are the Principals of two schools that stand no farther than two miles from each other. Both schools pool children from the 'better' part of town, so the demographic is almost entirely Caucasian, middle-to-upper-class and the schools' ranking is among the highest in the surrounding area. The parents of both schools are notoriously self-interested and demanding - being mostly Caucasian and upper-to-middle-class - and are known for having problems with virtually everything, meddling blindly in all matters regarding their precious offspring. The families of the children are so active they even have a Grandparents' Day, wherein the children spend the day with their parents' parents. Contrast this with the Elementary Schools on the South Side of our town, where the teachers inform me that during Parent Night, neither the parents *nor* the kids show up, leaving the teachers to sit around and chat amongst themselves. Sometimes, I'm told, someone brings in a movie and they watch that instead.

The time I spent at each of these schools was ridiculously minimal compared to the other schools I frequented. Out of my entire first year of substituting, I had spent exactly one (1) day at the A— Elementary School with Mrs. Tweedle-Dee and two (2) days at the H— Elementary School with Mrs. Tweedle-Dum. Those three days of substituting took place within a two-week period and I was mistakenly under the impression they would be 'easy' days because the kids in the schools actually wanted to be there and would therefore not be a handful to keep quiet. They were more or less the "gifted" schools of the area, at least when compared to the low test scores of some of the others.

The first time I went to H— Elementary, I tried getting in the side and back doors but they were locked. After walking around to the front of the building and in the door, I went into the office and remarked to the woman standing behind the counter that the school was "locked up like Fort Knox." She huffed and said that was for the protection of the children and that if I knew any better, I wouldn't have bothered trying to go in the side or back doors. This woman was Mrs. Tweedle-Dum, and I had already made a fantastic first impression.

The class I had was 5th grade, and the day went seemingly well up to a point. One of the other 5th grade teachers there, who I will call Mr. Beret - because of his tendency to wear such an object on his bald head - would wander in every once and a while and pace around the room. I asked him if he needed something and he said no, nothing in particular. Anyway, there was this stain in the back of the room on the floor - that of yellow paint. I asked the kids how the yellow paint got there, and they informed me that not too long ago, (then) local Representative Pat Toomey (R) made a special appearance and had some sort of demonstration for the class involving paint, but spilled most of it on the floor. One of the girls in the class said to me, "Don't you think it was stupid of him to pour the paint on the floor?" I agreed, and said that since he didn't take precautions by putting newspaper on the floor, that was quite careless. While an innocent response, this would come up to get me later on.

At another point in the class, I had to pass out issues of the Scholastic Weekly magazine, a "newsletter for kids" (most people under a certain age would remember these if they saw them; I certainly do) that happened to have a picture of George W. Bush on the cover. We read through the issue as a class and I let them do the exercises on the back for fun. Having finished early, one of the boys in the class cut out the picture of George W. Bush's face on the cover, with devil horns cut out along with it and various crayon marks on the picture itself. He raised his hand, I called on him, and he put the cutout over his face and went "Mwooohooohaaahaaa!" Call me juvenile, but I thought this was funny. Others started scribbling over the front cover photo the same as him - which isn't atypical for children to do (they always copy each other in things like this) - and waving around the defaced papers. I was still smiling, but told them to stop, because we had more work to do. They stuffed the mangled Scholastic Weeklies into their desks, and the day went on as usual. Mr. Beret continued to peek in the door, but after a while I just ignored him.

The next time I substituted was at A— Elementary School for 5th grade. After I signed in and went to the classroom, I found the other 5th grade teachers huddled in the room. I told them who I was and that I was filling in for the day, and they told me that there were no sub plans and that they were going to make some up for me. This is fine, I thought, at least I didn't have to wing it and manufacture tasks for the class. So far, so good.

When it came to the teacher's prep time - the time when the students go to either art, music, gym or a 'specialist' class - I wandered down the hallway to the faculty room. I was in there alone, reading a book I brought with me, when one of the 5th grade teachers that I spoke with earlier (she helped 'make up' the sub plans) told me that I shouldn't be in the faculty room at all or "spending work time reading." I set the book down and asked why. She told me that if the Principal, Mrs. Tweedle-Dee, came in, it wouldn't be pretty and that I should leave. She promptly went to the refrigerator for her lunch and left with me.

On the way back to the classroom, we talked for a little, and she said she wanted to bid out of the school because she didn't like the conditions she had to work under. She told me that the other teachers ate their lunches in their classrooms to avoid having an encounter with Mrs. Tweedle-Dee, who had a legendary bad temper. I asked why she or the other teachers never lodged complaints with the teacher's union or Human Resources. She told me that they did and that nothing could be done to 'remove' the woman - once anyone attains the title of Principalship (at least in the District I was in), that was it: that person was rendered a demigod, untouchable by any means and irreproachable.

The lesson plans were sketchy - it had the kids doing long division in preparation for a math test the following day, but they seemed utterly baffled by the instructions I provided. Without a math textbook to refer to - the regular teacher must have had it with her, because it wasn't in the room - I tried to figure out how they were taught and show them how I was taught. This only confused them further. I mean, I knew how to do long division and I thought there was only one way to go about it. After the math class was over, I felt *I* needed a tutor.

The following week I returned to H— Elementary. This time, however, Mrs. Tweedle-Dum was waiting for me. I signed in the office and found the 3rd grade class I was in for, but before I put my coat and bagged lunch down in the room, she was standing next to me, telling me that we were going to have a very serious discussion. The tone taken by her towards me was even more belittling than the way you would speak to an actual 3rd grader, and irked by this fact, I told her that I didn't like her tone. This was an immediate mistake. She went on to say that I was spouting 'liberal rhetoric' and 'preaching politics' to a group of 11-year-olds in the class I conducted the day before. I asked her to clarify. She said that one of the students told her parents that I called Representative Pat Toomey "stupid" and that the class told their teacher that I called President George

W. Bush "the devil." I tried clarifying what happened and how I tried to handle it, but she was unconvinced and appeared to have even more ammunition: I was asked, "Why did I permit the students to deface President Bush's face?" and "Why was I talking about Representative Pat Toomey at all?"

The meeting ended and she left me by pointing a finger in my face and telling me, "You know where we stand." I then spouted back, "This isn't Harvard, it's a grade school. Take it easy." This sealed my fate, and after being on the receiving end of what felt like Medusa's Glare, she stormed out of the room and slammed the door behind me. I finished the day, amidst foul classroom odors (something in the radiator, I guessed), one particular super-sick student (see Chapter 4 on Physical Illness) and, I'm not kidding you, thirteen (13!?) pages of lesson plans, which I did my best to adhere to. In total, I felt physically drained the whole day because of the early confrontation. And for what? I didn't care about the job, but I admit that I'm not always up for verbal altercations or getting cornered (it's obvious she planned *that* all along). Since my Mom was working in Human Resources, I had a feeling all day something was going to drift back to the office by Mrs. Tweedle-Dum, who's not the type to simply let things pass by.

Naturally, that internal hunch was correct. Herr Director of Human Resources, in what I was told was an "unprecedented move," told the Sub Callers to never call me again. My Mom, who was in the HR office and of course caught wind of all of this, was embarrassed. What happened was that Mrs. Tweedle-Dum called him personally and complained about me, and got, of all people, Mrs. Tweedle-Dee - who I never met and, following the advice of a regular teacher, stayed away from - to go in with her, both demanding my immediate removal. Herr Director said that if I wanted to keep my job, I had to have a meeting with him and the two women to "iron things out." I refused. Come on: It would have been three against one. So I told him I would only speak with him.

Everyone in the Human Resources Department knew about this, so when I came into the office to talk to him, I passed my Mom and all the other women she worked with. He sat me down and began reading from the letters from each of the two Principals. Mrs. Tweedle-Dum accused me of the aforementioned "political ranting," as well as "abrasive backtalk" and "not following the lesson plans." Mrs. Tweedle-Dee faxed a "Response Sheet" from the teacher I filled in for - remember, the one *without* the lesson plans - who claimed that I didn't "follow the lesson plans" and that I told, and this *really* hurts, "off-color jokes." Not following the lesson plans when there were no lesson plans and the lesson plans that *were* there were written by other teachers - okay, you got me on that - but the comment about "off-color jokes" hurt. I thought: *what off-color jokes?* I then became paranoid that I said something wrong, and searched my brain: what did I say? When did I say it? Herr Director must have noticed the mortified expression on my face, because I had to have looked like I was going to pass out. I told him I would never, ever do such a thing. He told me that the classroom teacher said that's what the children in the class said I did. I kept racking my brain trying to figure out what could have been said, and came up with nothing. My face flushed and I started shaking, giant pansy that I am.

Herr Director, feeling generous or pleased with himself for having brought me in and belittled me, said I could go back to substituting, but I could not return to those two schools, A— Elementary and H— Elementary. I was told by the then-Sub Caller, who quit a year later, fed up with him and the bitchy Principals, that she never had that happen before - that someone was just pulled off the list like that. She speculated that he wanted to prove a point with my Mother, who worked there and he never really liked. I was personally appalled that even if I had said those things, calling so-and-so an idiot, wasn't I allowed? Isn't that the First Amendment? Heaven forbid, defensive parents, your little darling ever hears anything derogatory about the Party and Belief System you have imposed on them. I can only chuckle in retrospect: wait until they turn 16 or so and start believing what they want to believe in.

After this incident, though, I was more paranoid than ever. I was afraid of being accused of things I hadn't done and had no way to prove I didn't do. I was also hurt inside, and made it a point to badmouth both of these people to every other substitute and teacher that would hear me out. I didn't care if they didn't want to hear it: I moaned anyway. What I found, in telling my little disaster story, that other people had similar problems with both of those Principals, not to mention a lot of the others I was lucky enough to have avoided up to that point.

One substitute, who had been doing it for *twenty-two years* (I call her "Old Sarge") and had seen it all, refused to go to H— Elementary because of her. She relayed to me a priceless anecdote at another school over coffee and yogurt: she was covering Library at H— two years ago. In the room were these Apple computers with software set up to search the contents of the library for the author or title of a desired book. Curious young boys will always be curious young boys, however, and some of the more seedy-minded 5th graders in her one Library session typed into the search engine some more "unsavory" terms. Old Sarge did not realize this at first – it took two of the girls from the class to come over to her and tattle. Old Sarge simply went over, turned off the computers, and told the offenders, "If you cannot behave correctly and use computers for learning you can't work on them." It was such a brief episode, she told me, and so minor in degree that she thought little of the whole incident. Hours later, during her lunch break, Mrs.

Tweedle-Dee came into the Teacher's Lounge and called *her* out into the hall. Mrs. Tweedle-Dee explained to Old Sarge that she just had three fifth grade girls come into her office to tell her about how "The Library Substitute did not handle the situation with the computers properly," and that the girls' homeroom teacher agreed with them, urging them to take it up with the Principal. When Old Sarge asked the Principal what she should have done, the Principal said, "Not what you did," and proceeded to espouse to great lengths on proper methods of correcting children.

Mrs. Tweedle-Dum had an equally loathsome reputation for berating her own teachers in front of their classes. One former teacher, back in Middle School and happier for it, would hear her heels clacking down the hallway and "actually shiver," expecting her to have a problem with something. Several times, he told me, she would stand but a few inches from him and shout *in his face*. He even told me the story about when a substitute came in, was so frustrated with her rather bratty class, couldn't get help from the neighboring teachers, stormed out of the room and went out to her car to go home. Mrs. Tweedle-Dum, on the verge of hysteria, ran outside, high heels and all, to scream at her to get back inside the building. He said he watched this from the hall, as did the other kids in the school. Talk about a glowing example of leadership!

One Substitute, who I'll call Mr. Carnegie (because he reminded me of a guy I knew who went to Carnegie Mellon), offered his advice. He spent a lot of time in some of the more, let's say 'elitist' schools outside the surrounding area, the ones from two-parent, high-income families and said he had a much easier time of it, at least *as a substitute* (he said he'd never, ever do it full-time). He said that though the children had attitudes, as expected, there was more a respect for authority and after he spent a good number of days filling in there, they even acknowledged him politely if they saw him in the hallway.

He told me when covering gym class at B— Middle School on the South Side of town, most of the kids didn't want to get "sweaty" so they defiantly sat on the floor during class - a "sit in" if you will - and downright refused to exercise. He had to call the office at the beginning of each class to get the Vice Principal over to "motivate" the kids to stand up and actually play kickball or volleyball or whatever indoor activity they were assigned to do. After a few classes of this, he got sick of calling the office, so he just pulled out a chair, let the kids on the floor while he read a book he brought with him. "It went much easier," he said.

Aside from suggesting I try some of the other school districts in the area, he also told me to take the same Zero Tolerance policy he always went with and never let up for a second. In other words, he didn't tolerate even a *minute* amount of B.S. Mr. Carnegie told me he would leap to the phone at a moment's notice and kick any kid out of the class. He also told me to never back down from anyone, not the teachers, not the kids ("You need to maintain dignity," I clearly recall him telling me, with regards to a job that doesn't necessarily feel dignified). One day, he was at N— Middle School, which has its share of problems and even a completely bizarre in-school suicide that took place years ago (details are hazy, but they found the body in the building) and there was a fight in the hallway. He stood there and saw it all happen, and another teacher eventually broke it up. The Principal of the Middle School, whom I'll refer to as Mrs. W., stormed over with her clacking heels, took all the kids from the hallway into the nearby gymnasium and asked Mr. Carnegie to go over to the gym with her. With the kids lined up in the room, she said, "Pick out the ones that started it." Mr. Carnegie looked around for the other teacher that broke up the fight and told Mrs. W. that he wouldn't know, and that she should bring over the other teacher to do that instead. Mrs. W. took Mr. Carnegie outside and began berating him about how the other teacher had "things she needed to do" and that Mr. Carnegie should have paid closer attention to the incident. He told me he stopped her dead in her tracks and got mouthy with her, telling her that he doesn't know the students, couldn't pick them out and that it wasn't his place to play detective. He said she was taken aback by this, and apologized to him for the tone taken and that was the end of it. When I appeared fed up and took a stand, I got myself into bigger trouble, but this man somehow stood his ground and was left alone (it might have helped that he was much older than me).

Certainly these domineering Principals are problems enough, but what do you make of, say, Assistant Principals paid well over $70k and can barely read over the intercom? Such was the case with the 8th grade Principal at E— Middle School, a former teacher elevated to a much more responsible position - when he had to go over the intercom and read the announcements, it came out like remedial 3rd grade reading. Some of the teachers, appalled that this man was given such a job - perhaps because of his race (he just so happens to be Hispanic … or is inferring that some people get their positions in America because of their minority status forbidden?) - and resentful, would actually call up each other over the phone or send each other instant messages over their computers to basically say, "Can you believe how dumb this guy sounds?" When I first heard him speak on the intercom, I asked the students who it was, thinking it was one of their classmates. One of them shrugged his shoulders and said, "I don't know, but I could read that better than he did."

3. The Trouble with Teachers.

Teachers are a skittish bunch. I've never known how to handle them, and until I've 'figured' certain ones out, I've remained especially guarded around them. I've found that a lot of them have this condescending tone that they adopt when I'm speaking with them outside the range of any students, but I've learned not to take it personally. Perhaps it's because the person they need to be for their day job leaks into all aspects of their persona: the need to command, to berate, to control. Elementary School teachers are predominately female because of the 'nurturing' aspects needed; Middle School teachers show an increase in males but still a lot of females (8th grade seems to have more male teachers than female teachers) and High School teachers are split somewhat evenly down the middle, 50-50.

Some teachers are fanatical and parent fearing, always worrying what class incident is going to come back to them in the form of a phone call or conference. Some are understanding to a fault. Some have taken me aside, assured me that I did a fantastic job, and told me not to worry about a thing. Others have harassed and followed me, wandered into the class I was teaching in, sat down at an empty seat and just watched me. (When I asked, in my own way, if he/she needed something, that person would just shake their head and say, "Just checking to make sure you're handling everything" which I never interpreted as helpful at all.) Some would offer unconditional support: I've been told by many kind souls that if I had a problem

with such-and-such problem kid to just send them next
door to their room and they'd find work for them;
inevitably, I had to call in that favor, because so-and-so
problem kid was *really* a disruption, calling me names or
rolling around on the floor. Some have told the Principals
to never let certain substitutes - including myself - into their
class again, which they have every right to do. I've always
wondered, what could possibly happen in one day? Did I,
just by my presence, ruin everything they'd been trying to
teach these kids up to that point? Was my mere existence -
or that of the other 'banned' teachers - simply that
devastating? Some do try to be helpful, but a few of the
well-wishers are patently delusional, like the one lady who
told me that the best way to control a class of "Emotionally
Disturbed" students was by feeding them Skittles.

I've been 'reprimanded' more by the teachers than by the
Principals, although the teachers carry less sway than the
Principals and their 'problems' with me were never major
enough to get me 'removed' from a school the way it had at
A— Elementary School and H— Elementary School.
Some of their comments were puzzling, and bear repeating.
One woman told me, point blank, that she thought I "sat
down" too much and needed to be more "pro-active" in
dealing with the class. I wasn't sure what she meant, so she
was too eager to explain. She had drifted past the room
several times during her 'free time' (which she must have
had a lot of) and every time she passed, at different
intervals during the day, I was sitting, at the desk, "writing
something" (her words). Let's see: the teacher's desk, in
this particular class on this particular day, was *in the front
of the room*, and the class had to do problems in their
textbook. What did she expect me to do? *Lean* over their
shoulder and make sure they understood each problem?
You know what the kids do when I walk around? They try
to make me do the work for them. They'll say, "Hey
meester, what's this?" and they'll point to the problem and

25

then I'll explain it - let's say it's reducing a fraction like 3/9 to simplest terms. I could talk up a storm, explain dividing the numerator and denominator by common terms, and they would look at me like nickels were falling out of my nose. Others would then have a similar problem. When I would go in front of the class and explain it, they'd try to follow along. I'd ask if they had questions. I'd give them more time to work on it. They still wouldn't get it, or pretend not to get it, or not care. Sometimes, they would pester me enough so that it became easier just give to them the answers or else start drawing pictures on the backs of the papers. Also, another deterrent from walking around the room was that they'd have their backpacks in the middle of the aisle and I would sometimes trip over them. The kids love to laugh at this, like I'm Chaplin and it's the amusement hour.

Some teachers have found me weeks after I've subbed in their room and said to me, "Were you in for me before?" I'd usually look at them puzzled, like *you mean back in October* and try to get at what they wanted. He/she would often say something like, "Did you remember to do the Social Studies work with the kids when you were in there? You didn't mark it down on your sub paper that you didn't and the kids said you didn't so I was just checking to make sure," and I'd just shrug my shoulders and think to myself are *you fucking kidding me*? I cannot tell you how often this had happened. I can't remember what shirt I wore the other day nor if I had the same colors on twice, and this person's trying to make me remember what I covered in his/her class countless class days if not weeks ago. I'd be so puzzled and irritated by this and my answers would be so vague and unhelpful that he/she'd usually let it go. I wanted to respond, "Do you know how many classes I've been in since then? What is this, a memory test?"

It is not uncommon for teachers to leave their rooms in utter chaos and expect me to figure out where everything is.

Take, for example, Mrs. Dull, a teacher at C— Elementary School. I was scheduled to work for her on the Wednesday and Thursday of one week. I found that there weren't any lesson plans, only her grade book open with the most obscure instructions. She had two teacher assistants in there that were supposed to 'help out' and 'know where everything was,' but both only compounded the problem by not being able to understand the lesson plans - which appeared to have been in hieroglyphics or short-hand - and had not a clue as to where the text books in the classroom were. Add to that the fact that the classroom was, in my opinion, a mess, with papers and glitter and glue and stacks of junk laying everywhere. It just so happened to be a "Learning Support" class, which meant that these very same students were the ones who struggled in their regular classrooms and had to be 'pulled' out every day to receive specialized - and 'slowed down' - learning material, and with not being very good *at* school, generally regarded school as absolute torture.

I put up with this disorder for Wednesday and Thursday and figured, well, I didn't get called by the Sub Callers for Friday, so that meant I had the day off. Well, my Mom, who was still working in Human Resources, called me around 9 AM, and told me that the secretary from C— Elementary School called *her* line, asking where I was. My Mom told her that I was only booked for that class on Wednesday and Thursday, and not for Friday. The secretary asked her to ask me - instead of calling me, at home, herself or going through the Sub Caller - if I would come in as soon as possible. So my Mom, caught in the middle of this, called me up and relayed all this to me over the phone. Obstinate as all hell, I refused, explaining that there weren't coherent sub plans, I couldn't find any of the text books, the classroom was a disorganized mess with glitter and garbage and the two teacher assistants couldn't find their asses with a map. Now, I love my Mom, but you know what she did? *She called up the school and told the secretary exactly what I said, word for word.* She didn't make an excuse, she didn't say I wasn't home, nothing simple like that. When I found out that she didn't 'lie' for me - I was speaking to Mom *in confidence* - I panicked. She told me not to worry about it, the secretary wouldn't say anything, it was no big deal. No one cared.

Technically, it wasn't a big deal. Yet, it got *ugly*. The Principal of the school was someone I've always gotten along with, and I thought I had a good rapport with the teachers there, but as soon as I went back to C— Elementary, it was anything but the same. No one would talk to me except for the secretary. I usually joked with the ladies in the Faculty Room about this and that, and I liked working there, but that was over, and it dawned on me what happened. Then, after I was returning from the faculty room with a cup of stolen coffee, none other than Mrs. Dull was leading her kids into the classroom. She spotted me, said to me, loaded with arrogance, "Are you Matt Lotti?" I just looked at her, not responding, and then she got loud: "Come and speak to me after school!" like I was one of her 3rd graders. Somewhat ready for this, I didn't just take it. I told her, "Absolutely not. You have a problem with me, you talk to the office, not *to* me" and walked away. It wasn't the office that had a problem with me, it was her, and I had a problem with her disorganization. The office knew where I stood - as did the rest of the teachers - but enough was enough. I didn't want her to get in trouble, but I didn't want to go back to her class, either.

A teacher's messiness hasn't always gotten me in trouble. Sometimes it causes others to boil over. Take for example, when I was at W— Elementary, and filling in for a Learning Support teacher (must be a pattern). Words cannot do justice to the nightmare that was her desk. It was piled with papers, worksheets, books, shelves, you name it. It looked like the custodian took several bags of recyclable paper, turned them over on the chair, floor and table and then just said, hey, I'm done here, and left searching for a sticky bun. I spent the first five minutes or so looking for sub plans or anything relating to my day's work, but nothing was there. I went back to the office to explain my dilemma, only the Principal was there. I told her there weren't any sub plans and the desk was a disaster. This sent her *right over the edge*. She strong-stepped it out of the office and over to the desk of horrors I was speaking of, took her arm and pushed every piece of junk *off* the desk and *onto* the floor. "There," she said, "now you have a clean desk." She went nearby and got another teacher. "Find something for him to do," she instructed this other woman, unaware of what was happening and then dropped what she was originally doing and helped me out. I felt good about this, and have always gotten along with her - that was a case of two personalities clicking together. Others claimed she was harsh and easily infuriated (a few teachers I knew from there left the school because of her), but from what I heard, the messy teacher had been warned several times about the unacceptable state of her workspace. And no, there was never any backlash towards me from this incident or any other incident, which meant I was all too pleased to return there.

This example illustrates another dimension to the complexity of the formula, one that doesn't appear clear at first but does once you've been around it: the endless stream of problems, the *cycle of problems*, that plague all involved. The Principals are on the teachers about the state of their classrooms, the way they handle their students, the grades the students are getting. The Principals get constant phone calls from parents - the more involved the parents are, the more phone calls they receive. The Principals have to set deadlines for their teachers to turn in paperwork, administer tests, etc. The Teachers have to handle all in-class crises, misbehavior, homework not being turned in, little girls complaining about how other little girls call them names, boys complaining they don't get called on enough not to mention actual teaching woes, like the need to get in so much information when innumerable external problems may arise, when the students don't understand the most basic of concepts, when test grades are low and students openly defy a system designed to push them through (one teacher whispered to me, "As long as they show up and do their homework, they'll pass"). It's remarkably stressful, although not in a "I was digging ditches all day" sort of way, but your body, sometimes, just gives out and all you want to do is lay down in a dark, quiet room and banish everyone from your sight. If you have never done it, it's impossible to describe: it's as if the mental stress translates into physical fatigue. It's rarely boring, which makes those who thrive on chaos love it all the more, but if you're not the type that likes to deal with constant problems and pressures *and* you have a challenging class of miscreants that you must deal with every day - children born of negligent parents, of phenomenally warped backgrounds - all day, for weeks on end, it's no wonder frustration and depression set in.

The statistics for teachers coming and going - getting hired and quitting - tells so very much. In what appears to be a famous and much-cited survey - so well-known that one Elementary School had it posted in the faculty room - conducted by *Education Week* showed that 20% of new teachers leave the classroom after three years and 50% leave after five years. I've even noticed that some of the teachers I knew and spoke with my first year were nowhere to be found by my third year. When I asked around where someone I subbed for in the past was, most looked at me suspiciously and acted as if it was none of my business. One female my age who subbed with me during my first year quit and went to Bartending School. I never asked why - even though I saw her a few times at a bar I frequent where I'm assuming she works - though I'm sure it's because bottles of gin are easier to handle than children.

I was once told that the attitude teachers take towards substitutes was directly proportionate to the years they'd spent as a teacher. The more years they've put in, the farther they were removed from the whole idea of substituting and therefore less sympathetic to those of us just being thrown into a strange situation for a day, not aware of the class' actual 'dynamic.' It also comes down to personality, as well: the one rude woman who worked at H— Elementary and left me a 13-page packet of sub notes - and then complained when I didn't 'finish it all' - was not the kind of person to give anybody a break. You can't reason with someone like that.

One commonly held belief is that teachers are notoriously underpaid for challenging work, and from the research I did on the national numbers, that isn't a myth. In general, the average starting salary in the United States for a teacher out of college with a basic teaching certificate is somewhere near $38k. The real incentives start coming in with tenure and additionally earned degrees - get a Master's Degree and stay with the District for five years and you'll get a pleasant boost in pay. But when I've asked teachers about this, they aren't overjoyed, and it's obvious why: after spending all day in school, the last thing they want to worry about are Graduate classes at night (when you want to put your feet up) not to mention finding time to do *their* own homework for school and do research for *their* term papers. In a comical example, I was called to work in a building that, as it turned out, didn't need any substitutes. Instead of sending me home with pay (which does happen if they call me to work in the morning and then tell me I can leave), they put me in the room with one of the regular teachers who wants help. It turns out that she has to work on her own 10-page term paper for class that night, was late, and needed to finish. She gave me some very basic work for the kids to do while she plunked away on her laptop; at lunch, she asked me to proofread it. In the afternoon, instead of pretending to have me run the class, we watched a Disney film, *The Emperor's New Groove*, and she kept typing.

A good portion of the teachers I've been friendly with have confided that they have side jobs that they do on the weekends or during the summers. When I asked why they didn't keep the summers off - a bona-fide perk of the profession - it's always because of money woes. Almost none of them told me, "Oh, that cosmetics counter gig at Macy's that I drive to after class on Friday? I just … you know, wanted to get out of the house." Some have spouses that were laid-off or had part-time jobs themselves - those multiple children and their doctor bills, mortgages, car bills, and credit card bills don't pay for themselves, and in a painfully rich country like America, even $36k isn't enough for these individuals. The idea of having a full-time teaching job, a part-time job and graduate classes sounds absurd, but some forge on and find time for all of them.

My Mother was a teacher. She put in six years for a now-defunct Catholic school on the South Side of our town. It came to the point where she had enough of the job and wanted to stay home and care for her newborn son (which would be me). She's never regretted leaving. She would tire of calls from parents, feel defeated by students who were failing and didn't get along with the older nuns who worked in the same building and treated her poorly because she was young (so poorly, in fact, that my Father and Grandmother had to have a talk with the administrations about the harassment). She doesn't regret leaving, either, and if she could go back to college she would have re-planned her career path. She should have gotten the message, back when she was in college back in 1972, to change majors when her Elementary Education professor committed suicide by turning her car on in the garage.

4. Everyone Loves a Good Vomit Story (or Two).

One thing to always count on while teaching is that you are going to become infected with every germ that enters the building. It's inevitable. A few smart teachers have anti-bacterial hand creams on their desk and maybe a bottle of Lysol spray on a shelf in the room, but they don't work. Why? Because one of the only ways I'd know they have anti-bacterial hand creams and Lysol spray *was if I was in a class for a teacher who had gotten sick*, and a good portion of the students were out, too. I hate to admit this, but I'm an obsessive hand-washer, and the fact that these greasy, unclean hands were handing me papers or borrowing my pen to sign out to go to the restroom or handing me sick notes from the doctor made me start to cook internally. I usually told the kids to put the papers on the desk or borrow someone else's pen, but there I'd be, two days later, sneezing and mainlining Motrin.

Adults, when they get quite ill, are able to run to the bathroom. Kids, for some reason, don't have that kind of self-control. Two incidents took place that were gross, foul and unpleasant, and keeping with the District status quo, handled with negligence by the staff. The timeliness of these incidents was impeccable, too, as they both took place at schools with less-than-tolerant attitudes towards pretty much everything. Apologies ahead of time to those with weak stomachs and to John Waters, the "Prince of Puke," for violating his territory.

At H— Elementary - yes, that school again, the one with Tyrant Queen Mrs. Tweedle-Dum - a little girl sitting right in the front of the room told me she didn't feel good. She had her head down on the desk and looked quite pale. I wrote a pass for her to go to the nurse, but she wouldn't go, she just wanted to put her head down. I wasn't satisfied with her answer, and pressured her. Children are often times good at playing sick, but this girl was certainly not pretending. After an hour of class time passed she didn't look any better. She told me she'd better go to the nurse. Handing her the note, she walked to the door and opened it. Then she stopped, with her back to the class, and paused in the doorway for what had to have been a half-a-minute, her head down. I turned to her and called her name, but she didn't respond. The rest of the kids were looking at her too. Next thing I know, she's throwing up all over the floor. I dashed over to her to see if she was okay, but she just slumped down and sat there. The color of the discharge was bright red - or to my less-than-perfect eyes looked bright red - and that's when I freaked, thinking it was blood and she was hemorrhaging internally or something nearly fatal. I ran down the hall to the office to tell them that this girl was sick, and that they should send someone. I was under the impression the color red was from blood - it never dawned on me it could have been fruit juice or candy. Mrs. Tweedle-Dum, who was in the office, *screamed* at me. "What are you doing in here? Why did you abandon your class? You should have used the classroom phone." I apologized - I hadn't expected this response - and went back to the room. Upon returning, and stepping over the mess and the sick girl - I was pleased that the rest of the children were still sitting there, not having been kidnapped or murdered in the two minutes I was out of the room. Trying to think up an excuse to pacify Mrs. Tweedle-Dum, I spotted the phone list of every number in the building - the phone list I admittedly should have seen and used to call the nurse - and, harried and desperate for an excuse, took it off the wall and stuffed it under some paperwork. Smart, Lotti, smart.

In about ten minutes - yes, ten minutes - the nurse did find her way over to the room and took care of the sick girl, whom she helped up and walked down the hallway. The custodian and Mrs. Tweedle-Dum both came over: the custodian cleaned up the mess, while Mrs. Tweedle-Dum found her way over to me and looked at the class phone. She asked where the phone list was. I told her I couldn't find it and that's why I didn't call the nurse directly, or something to that extent, and she wandered around the room looking for it. She couldn't care less that there was a girl really sick or anything like that. After our "morning conversation," she was looking for something else to get at me with - ironically, the sick child was not her concern ... berating *me* was. I admit I should have used the class phone to call the nurse, and hiding the phone list was profoundly juvenile on my part. But I thought the girl was *seriously* ill. Forgive me for caring just a little. Mrs. Tweedle-Dum, if she were any kind of person, could have taken me aside and put it more kindly - "You really shouldn't leave the class," and so on - but that would involve a certain kind of honorable character, which this woman failed to possess.

C— Elementary School was the scene of the second vomiting episode. I was covering for a 5th grade class, and one girl in the back of the room - in this room, the desks were arranged in five equal rows - put her face down on her desk and threw up over it so hard, it cascaded all over her desk *and* the desks of some of the kids sitting adjacent to her. Kids are kids, and those around her flipped out, jumped out of their seats and shrieked. I tried calming everyone in the room down, sent the girl down to the nurse and then called the office (this was the second time, so I was much more composed; the discharge was also not red).

I did my best to do crowd control and move the kids around until the custodian could come in and clean up the mess. Even after the floor was mopped, the kids didn't want to return to their desks, and understandably so.

In an hour, after my 50-minute break period (the kids were in art class), I returned to the room to find the same girl back in her seat. I was puzzled. I talked to the girl and asked her why she was back in the room and she said the nurse was trying to call her parents. She looked even more ghostly than before. I asked if she had a temperature and she said she didn't know. Perplexed, I continued on with whatever was written in the sub plans.

Before I knew it, I heard a gulp and the girl threw up on her desk *again*. The kids were part disgusted and part jovial, yelling, "She did it again!" Again, I sent her down to the nurse and again, I called the office to send the custodian. The custodian asked me if it was the same girl. I told him it was. He asked me what the girl was doing back in class. I told him what the girl told me. He cleaned it up and I moved the kids affected by the sickness to 'buddy up' with partners elsewhere in the class.

You may not believe it, but in about twenty minutes, *she was back in the room*. Another 5th grade teacher was right next-door and had been following this whole episode with me. I asked the girl what happened; she said the nurse sent her back. At lunchtime, the regular 5th grade teacher and I went into the office to find out what was going on. The secretary told us to talk to the nurse. The two of us went into the nurse's room and asked why she didn't keep the girl in *her* office, who was clearly very ill. The nurse told the both of us that she couldn't get the girl's father on the phone, and that when he would arrive to pick her up, she'd call me. I asked the nurse why she didn't keep her in the room away from the kids. She said, "Why should I keep her in here? I don't want to get sick too." I'm not even sure the word "incredulity" fits in this situation. In case you're wondering, *no*, the girl's father never picked her up and she stayed in the classroom until the end of the day. Mercifully, she didn't make any further messes (perhaps because she didn't eat lunch).

To combat attendance problems, the U.S.' No Child Left Behind Act says that students must have a fever of 101.5 or have vomiting/diarrhea before he/she can go home - supposedly the number of kids leaving for 'minor illnesses' was too great. The kids have found their own way around this fever 'limit' - a few told me that they were genuinely sick but didn't have a fever as high as 101.5, so they went into the bathroom and made 'retching sounds' and then were allowed to leave. I don't know about most people, but there have been times when my fever never hit 101 and I felt like I couldn't move, or had a severe sinus infection. I've sent kids to the nurse who have been sent back and put their heads down and as long as they weren't throwing up, I just left them alone. The decree is also a built-in way to make the nurses' lives easier - instead of pretending to know what they're doing and actively deciding if the child is faking illness or genuinely ill, they just check the temperatures and make the decision from there.

Just as teaching is not an easy job, I imagine neither is nursing, but sometimes all one needs is just a little common sense. At L— Elementary, there was a school assembly wherein the Principal wanted to speak to the students about some pressing matter (I don't recall what, exactly - behavior on the buses, maybe?) and after her announcement there was an hour-long musical interlude by one of the Middle School bands and all the kids sat on the floor to listen. After this interruption first thing in the morning (a gift for a substitute: trust me), I walked the class I was with back to their room. Upon returning, one of the boys in the class alerted me to one of the girls in the class - since it was September she was wearing shorts, and her legs were covered with blood. I thought she was having her period or something - female trouble - and I asked her if she wasn't "feeling well," but she seemed relatively composed. Not sure of what happened - I was afraid to delve, at this point in my 'teaching career' - I sent her to the nurse to get cleaned up.

In about twenty minutes I received a phone call from the nurse. She told me that the girl was intentionally scratching open the skin on her legs to make them bleed. I told her it sounded abnormal and that there could be a major problem. The nurse told me she "bandaged her up" and that if there were further issues, that was for "the parents to sort out." When the girl came back to the room, she had - and I did count - *one* small Band-Aid on each leg, only partially covering the numerous gashes in the skin from the girl's nails. Some traces of dried blood were still visible on her legs. For the rest of the day, she kept picking at it, and the blood naturally found its way around the tiny bandages, but it was evidently none of my business and I tried to ignore her. Obviously the nurse didn't think enough to talk to the school counselor or even *properly cover the wounds*, and there was nothing more I could do. Was I the only one that saw that self-mutilation was a sign of a deeper problem? Or was I overreacting, and the girl was just itchy? I did ask the girl if she felt okay, and she said yes, so maybe it all meant nothing. If it did mean something, the girl will have to keep looking for someone to start caring.

5. Caught in the Funhouse Part I: Student Behavior in Elementary School.

When not dealing with some form of administration and their concerns, the most pressing problems typically originated with the students themselves, and as you may imagine, these problems start quite early. Teachers in the fourth and fifth grades hear well ahead of time about the proverbial boils still forming in kindergarten and first grade, so in a perverse way (that is, pending retirement or transferring to another building), they are able to foresee their own teaching future. Perhaps in those few years, if a potential menace is present, those teachers can pray really hard some of the terrible infants will transfer schools because their parents are constantly moving for whatever financial reason. It happens often, actually.

It's as clear as day, this teacher-student situation: the teacher is the surrogate parent. Neglected, abused children don't always come to class in the right state of mind, and it's up to the teacher to manage this for several hours of several days of several weeks and so forth. Sometimes "action plans" are created for the especially difficult, but to me, it seems, once you get stuck with a particular student, he/she is going to be there. "Removing" them from the school via referrals doesn't always work.

Now, as a substitute, every single day is different: different classes, different schools, different circumstances, different lesson plans. Adjusting to these changes regularly is quite trying: tactics that may work in one school in quelling the storms don't necessarily work in another school where the students are immune to negotiations and do not fear reprisals. All schools have varied internal mechanisms that need to be deciphered like the Enigma Code: some frown upon strict behavioral discipline ("kids will be kids") while others actually appear to have grown irritated with me for a 'laid-back' approach when they're expecting me to fill out behavioral reports and send the problem kids to the main office. It's important to discern the two: often times, students determined to disrupt everything I do, after being sent to the office, are sent back. When I call the office and ask why the boy/girl was sent back to the room, I was usually told by the secretary that I should just "hold onto" the student for the time being, because they had meetings or parents or too many kids in the office. I would then take matters into my own hands and send the problem outside and out of eyeshot (this is important: they'll often make faces or lewd gestures in the hallway) and shut the door. I was told this was unacceptable disciplinary practice in Elementary School, but I did not care.

A lot of my very toughest days were with some defiant, rude and contemptible Elementary School students. It's well known that the students can be difficult for their own teachers, but when they see a substitute come in, their eyes light up. Heaven. In some ways, it's like having the Ring of Gyges for them: that magical device (mentioned in Plato's *Republic*) that, if you turn it in a certain direction, you become invisible and can do anything you want, to your heart's desire. No one ever figures that I'll write their names down to their teacher (all substitutes must fill out a sub report and hand it in to the office, though the office staff just throws it in the teacher's mailbox) - in fact, when I *tell* them I'm writing their names down for their teacher, it usually comes as a surprise, and the whole room gets quiet. *You mean you can tell Mr./Mrs. X I was bad? I hadn't thought of that!* Well no kidding, you're 10. In another

41

dozen years you can be in my shoes, writing up names too. It's not a relief, I can assure you.

Whether or not anything is done to them is up to the teacher, and the level of punishment varies greatly. In Elementary School, I'm afraid to report, it involves a stern talking to, but tragically enough, it often involves an interrogation ... of *me*. If I should be unfortunate enough to be in the same building the next day, and this has sadly happened (though I've always tried to avoid going to the same school on consecutive days for precisely that reason), the teacher would often find me and inquire as to why I wrote names down, and exactly what they did. Now, I always tried to write a basic description of the misbehavior on the form for the teacher, and that by finding out the details of what happened is the regular teacher's job, but in the time between dismissal of the previous day and the opening bell of the next day, there was no guarantee I would remember the exact things he or she did. Very often, to my surprise and disappointment, the teacher would say, "But [boy/girl] would *never* do that!" when I gave a very basic rundown of what transpired. It was like they became the parent instead of the surrogate parent, and were getting as defensive as if it were their own child. I would insist that I had no desire to make up false information about any students, that I did not have any invested interest in who gets rewarded and who gets punished. If I wrote an infraction down, it was because that's precisely what I saw.

These same teachers would also neglect to inform me of some relatively important matters - primarily, which of their students had severe emotional disturbances. You would think that I, as a fill-in teacher, would be 'tipped off' about this, but it almost never happened. I did not expect a personal conference, but a heads-up might have been nice. One girl, in the 2nd grade at D— Elementary - whom I can never forget - had to have had *countless* things wrong with her – things you can tell just by watching her for a little bit.

She talked to herself endlessly, laughed at things that weren't there, cried at a moment's notice and refused to follow any form of direction. She would pester the other kids, and no one wanted to sit with her. I tried to move them away to promote peace, but she'd simply get up and wander around, getting into mischief and drawing my attention away from everything else I was trying to accomplish.

When it came time for their class' bathroom break - in some Elementary Schools, they have specially timed breaks during which they line up in the hallways and wait their turn to go while in other schools, the classes have bathrooms built into them - she was the first one in (she made sure of it), and after a couple of minutes passed, one of the other girls that was in there came over to me to tell me she wouldn't come out. I sent the same little girl back in so that she'd tell the other girl to come out of the bathroom. That didn't work, either. Embarrassed, I had to ask a nearby (female) teacher to step out of the class she was trying to conduct to do something about it, and she was quite gracious, going into the bathroom herself. Upon bringing her out - and she had to be *steered* out, like a wild, swerving car - the other teacher told me that the girl was in one of the stalls, screaming the words "*American Standard*" (the manufacturer who made the toilets) repeatedly. The other kids in the class, seeing and hearing this, were understandably unnerved. On another occasion, this same teacher told me, the disturbed girl was shouting the words "*Captain Crunch*," because, they surmised, that's what she had for breakfast.

Another day, in the same 2nd grade class, this same bizarre girl was still in there, and in the afternoon portion of the day she had managed to shove a mechanical Bic pencil into the webbing of her hand (in between the thumb and forefinger), and was screaming and carrying on from the pain. I sent her to the nurse with an escort (another, frankly more sane, little girl). Five minutes later, they both returned - all the nurse had done was pull out the pencil and put a giant Band-Aid over the wound. I alerted the special education teacher of her behavior, who informed me that the school recommended this poor girl be tested for autism and/or schizophrenia months ago, but nothing was sent back from the pediatrician (or psychiatrist) to the school. Until they heard something, she told me they'd have to just "let it go."

That girl was calm compared to a demented little boy in the 3rd grade at C— Elementary, who also had a history of mental "breakdowns." He sat quietly through the first few hours of school, doing whatever work I wrote on the board or reading along in the book, but when it came to snack time - which was supposed to 'tide' them over until lunch - he changed. Most kids have their own snack - their parents pack them - but in the cases where the kids don't have snacks, the teacher would supply them with something to eat. This boy, along with a few others, didn't have his own, and so - as per the directions on the sub plans - they each got two cookies from the box that the classroom teacher had. When everyone finished eating their snacks, he came up to me and told me I should give him more cookies because he was "good." I reiterated that everyone received two cookies, and that's all. This was unsatisfactory to him, and he started slamming his hands on the desk. "That's not fair! I was good!" he yelled. Not willing to give in to a temper tantrum, I walked away from him and started with the new lesson. But he wasn't willing to let it go. His own peers were tired of his yelling, and two of the boys - in particular - told him to stop it. His anger became redirected at them, and he stood up and ran across the room, yelling at them and slamming his hands on the desk. They got up, ran in the back and he followed. I then intervened, told him I was calling the office, and that's when he ran past me into the in-class bathroom (some do have it, so that the kids

44

don't have to have bathroom breaks in the hallways like they do at other schools) and locked the door and started kicking the walls.

The Principal was out, so one of the other teachers who had a free period came over and talked him out of the bathroom. Later on in the day, the teacher asked me to write down what happened. He specifically asked me if there was a 'trigger' that set him off, and that 'trigger' was obviously food. When I tried asking questions, like *why did that boy become hysterical*, for example, the teacher wouldn't say and dodged my obvious concerns. Didn't I have a right to know? Later that same day, after lunch, the kids told me that the temperamental boy had a 'fit' in the cafeteria, slamming his plastic tray with food around and 'attacking' the lunch tables before he had to be physically restrained. The kids told me - and here's the punch line - it happened 'all the time.' Perhaps the second punch line was that the children knew more of what was going on than I did.

Sometimes, I became the target of rage. At M— Elementary School (one that has a lot of kids from low-income, largely minority families), I was in a 4th grade class and a boy was acting up. I had corrected him countless times throughout the day, but to no avail. I moved his desk, I wrote his name on the board, I even sent him to other rooms with other teachers (who would send him back in about twenty minutes). Eventually, I gave the class busywork (worksheets) and went to the teacher's desk in the corner of the room to look for the next assignment to give the class, which was when this boy came up to me and asked me if he could have his toy out of the desk. I didn't understand what he was saying, and the other kids told me that if they were caught playing with a toy after being warned several times to put it away, it went into the June Drawer, meaning it wouldn't be until June that they were given their confiscated objects back. I told him - and the

45

rest of the class - that it wasn't up to me to take objects out of the teacher's desk, and that I wasn't the person to ask. In typical teacher fashion, I also told him to go back to his seat and go back to work.

I wasn't really paying attention to where he went after that, but the next thing I know, I see this object hurled at me and hit me in the shoulder/neck area (right on the left collar of my shirt) and fall down to the desk. The kid - and I don't know where he found it - threw a *ceramic tile* at me. It didn't shatter or break - it hit my neck and then fell right on top of the desk. Everyone in the class started laughing, but especially the boy who wanted his toy back. I examined the tile and asked who threw it. Everyone pointed to the boy who gave me trouble all day. I asked him if he did it - and where he got it - but he just kept laughing. So I screamed - and I *screamed* - "*That's it, we're going to the office right now.*" I walked out the class to the next door teacher, explained to her what happened, and she told me if I'd cover her class she'd take him to the office.

When she came back after having dropped the boy off, she told me that I should go to the office to fill out a Code of Conduct form, writing out what happened, and that I should call his parents. Me? Call parents? I went to the office, and of course the Principal and Vice-Principal were nowhere to be found, but the secretary, a very kind woman, helped me fill out the forms and called the parents herself. She told me my neck was red, which I expected, and that I should have been grateful it didn't hit my face. I went back to the room to get the Exhibit #1, the tile, and take it to the office. I tried not to let everyone know how infuriated I was at this child's behavior. At the very least, everyone in this case proved quite supportive, which made it sting considerably less.

A similar incident occurred at F— Elementary (another school known for its large percentage of students from low-income housing), in the 3rd grade, only this sad occurrence

46

did not involve products you could find at Home Depot to refurbish your bathroom floor. Another problem student, another long, depressing day ... I used every trick in my book to calm this short, angry boy down, but he refused to sit or listen. I put his desk in the hallway but he kept coming back in. Other teachers would stop in to yell at him - a few took him for a spell to give him work to do. He started bickering with the other kids in class, and would antagonize them by wandering around the room, knocking things off their desks.

One of the boys in the class didn't like having his things pushed off the desk and stood up and shoved him lightly. The troubled kid ran over to me, telling me that the other kid "attacked" him and the other kid should be punished by me. Irritated at this point, I told him no, I saw what happened, and then I said if he didn't sit down I was going to send him out of the room again. He repeated his demand, telling me to send the other kid out of the class, and not him (this is not uncommon: they insist and insist, like I'm their parents saying 'no' to a toy they want). Once again, I refused. Then he did the unthinkable: he spit in my face. I was sitting at the teacher's desk and he just spit at me and then stomped away to his seat. Stunned, I cleaned off my face with my handkerchief, and then made a phone call to the teacher next door. I sent him out again.

A week later, I was back at the same school and yes, he was still there.

The spitting was just an example of the kind of disgust and disregard some students have for teachers. Granted, I was only a substitute, which is truly the lowest of the low, but when I relayed the story to someone else at another Elementary School, it didn't surprise her. She told me of a friend of hers who taught in Middle School and had a female student smack her in the face. At least you can wipe spit off.

I've often wondered whether or not all of this comes down to a kind of collective mental illness, or a crack in the word "respect," a word which gets thrown around a lot probably because it's so very lacking. I can certainly roll out the stories of what I can only deem lunatic behavior - one boy at F— Elementary School unzipped his jeans, placed a twig he found outside in his pants and then "pretended" to fornicate with the fence outside the school ... and then he chased around his classmates at recess with it jutting out, "poking" them. One girl, when she was told she couldn't do whatever it is she wished (get a drink, go to the office, call her Mom), pulled out her hair until there was blood at the end of her blonde locks and fingertips. There was a boy at N— Elementary who 'charged' at a girl drinking at the water fountain, knocking her teeth into the porcelain and dislodging them. I remember countless kids in Elementary School who would have to leave at certain times during the day to go to the nurse to get their daily meds for ADHD or ADD. Then, there would be those kids who were, to quote their teachers, "being tested" for ADHD or some other disability. And then there would be the ones who just wanted attention, to alleviate boredom, to earn the *respect* of their peers at my expense (and the expense of their regular teachers). There's that word again.

6. Caught in the Funhouse Part II: Student Behavior in Middle School.

My first year of teaching was devoted exclusively to the Elementary Schools. I was trying to get accustomed to the style; I didn't want to be fumbling around in the Middle and High Schools in front of those adolescents (it's okay when they're eight years old; sixteen year olds tend to be more observant and critical). I was scared off by the conversations I had with other subs that covered middle and highs. "Either do elementary or High School. Don't even step *foot* in Middle School," I was already warned by one knowledgeable individual. I followed this advice at first, but got curious, and wound up surrounded by the hormonal blues.

Some of the pleasant constants of Elementary School seemed to be negated in Middle School. Being older, it was more difficult to subdue or threaten them. Having spent time in the system longer, they were much more clever and tried everything in their power to trick and deceive in order to get out of class or get out of doing their work. Launched into those depressing, awkward teenage years, it's a headache for them and me: attitudes develop, crushes are formed, fights are a lot more frequent, school becomes more of a burden.

Middle School is also the first time the classes are actively separated by intellect, at least in the schools I frequented. There were the A-track kids, who were the brightest, I suppose, then the B-track, then B.I.-track (which stands for B-track 'Integrated' because they refuse to use the term 'C-track,' which the slower students might find 'demoralizing' - incidentally, almost all Middle School teachers refer to them as 'C-track' anyway) and sometimes a Special Ed. class would sneak into the rotation, or even an ESOL (English as a Second Language) class (each school seems to create their own unique units, so none of the four Middle Schools I went to were arranged exactly the same). It would be rational to think that the A-track kids, being smarter, would be better students to work with, but it's the B-track kids that I always found most accommodating. Often times, A-track kids were the biggest wise-asses who knew everything and were the ones to tell *me* how things were going to be done - their lack of respect for anyone was often repellant (being A-track apparently anointed them as 'kings') and even after I would *yell* at them to stop talking - it would never be just one or two talking, it would be the whole class - they would continue on as usual. It was the equivalent of taunting. Try and stop us.

The B.I./Special Ed./ESOL students were often quite a different problem, and though some of their class sizes were smaller, it was just as difficult to watch over them. One B.I.-Track class that I had in my fourth year of teaching (at M— Middle School) consisted of about fourteen kids sitting at six round tables (immediately a problem I noticed, walking in the door - sitting close to each other merely encourages chattering plus there's the logistical issue of where to move the problem students). One of the girls, and I was warned about her ahead of time, decided she was going to start crawling around the floor and grabbing people's feet. I told her to sit down and she did, but as soon as I turned my back she was on all fours again. The rest of the class was no better - they weren't crawling on the floor, but they were playing musical chairs and switching seats and moving around. While I tried to corral the rest of them and get them seated, this girl ran up to me, screaming and crying. She put her hand in front of her face and was trying to show me her cut finger - apparently, while she was crawling around the floor, one of the boys in the class (who was wandering around belligerently) stepped on her hand "accidentally." She was wearing a giant ring on the hand that got stepped on, a ring with what looked like spikes sticking out of it, the spikes scratched up her finger. She demanded to go to the nurse. I told her I didn't see any blood and that she should go sit down - honestly, I didn't take a very good look at the finger and was more intent on calming her down - she started yelling at me and waving her hand more, saying that she was injured and that she *had* to go to the nurse. I took a second look at the hand and sent her down - and truthfully, removing her from the class for any period of time was a relief.

The craziness of her crawling simultaneously escalated when I had to have a conversation with another teacher who heard about the girl scratching her finger, and decided to talk to me about it while standing out in the hallway at the end of the day. She asked me exactly what happened, and I told her. She then said to me, and these are the exact words, "Why did you let her crawl on the floor?" I thought about the way she phrased the statement and responded, "I didn't *let* her do anything. She just *crawled*." The teacher shook her head, but I was unsure as to whether or not I should have been offended. What was she getting at, me *letting* her crawl on the floor!? I explained that I kept correcting her *repeatedly*, and even sent her out of the room to stay with another teacher because she wouldn't listen to what I was saying. What was I to do, pick a 13-year-old girl off the floor and tie her to her chair? Oh, and did I mention this girl's father was in jail and that she was already in trouble - legally, with the school - for stealing a teacher's belongings?

Surprisingly, M— Middle School was supposed to be one of the "better" area Middle Schools - the Elementary

Schools that feed into it are from "better" neighborhoods (this is what I was told) - but one of the most frustrating and, might I add, infuriating incidents I had to deal with took place there, with me and relatively intelligent (meaning A-track) but snide 7th grade kids. Just when I thought I was getting a handle on things, I was thrown out of the vehicle.

The set-up is a tad involved, so it requires a little briefing. Under what's called the Skill 21 initiative, students - at least in the local District, anyway - were given their own personal laptops to use throughout the day, free of charge. Yes, you heard me correctly: every student in Middle School was given his/her own laptop to take from class to class. Many outsiders bristle when they hear this, and perhaps correctly: *millions of tax dollars went towards buying teenagers computers* (most non-teachers I talked to about this inevitably asked me, "What, aren't books good enough?"). The computers have programs on it for them to type their papers or do research, but they were often used to play 'educational games,' like something called First In Math, which we used to play using primitive cardboard cards when I was in school, way, way back in the dark ages. World Book Encyclopedia was on the laptops, but the kids often just used them to torment me by playing the accompanying sound files on it very loudly (lions roaring, the National Anthem, etc.). So yes, essentially, young teenagers were purposely being held responsible for a thousand dollar machine that they (mostly) played games on.

I was filling in, for a two day stretch at M— Middle School, for the same Reading teacher. This one class I had (which I'll just denote 7-A to make it easier), when their class ended, would leave their laptops and backpacks in the room and go to lunch. Once lunch was over, they'd return to the room, pick up their belongings and go to their next class. Although it was never explicitly stated, I, as the room teacher, was held responsible for the room - I had to make sure the door locked if I left during that time so no one could get in. However, since I didn't have a key - the teacher I was filling in for didn't have one and the office couldn't give me one - I stayed in the room and ate my lunch in there, making sure the door was shut. Before eating, I called my Mom (who, by this time, had already left Human Resources and was working in the Information Technology Department), looked out the window, and slowly ate my sandwich and orange.

Once the kids came back from lunch, I opened the door, and they rushed in to get their computers and backpacks to go to their next class. Remember: I was the only one in the room while they were at lunch. So, after the first wave of kids came in, got their belongings and left, a few stragglers came in afterwards. One of them came up to me and said, "I can't find my laptop." He told me it was on his desk when he left, but it was gone (this kid deserves a name, since he becomes a central figure later on - I'll dub him Dodo); I agreed with him, saying I saw it on his desk (it was in the back corner of the room, and when I made the phone call I saw it was there) and that he should ask his classmates where it went.

Apparently, he didn't ask his classmates anything, he went straight to the office and came right back up with the Vice Principal. She pulled me away from the class I was teaching and asked me a half-dozen questions about where I was when the laptop went missing. She was visibly irate, and I was uncomfortable. I told her what I knew, and she left for a bit. When I came back, one of the kids in the class said, "Man, she acted like you were responsible," which may have been the student trying to goad me, but I didn't respond.

In less than five minutes, the Vice Principal returned, this time with the school police officer, who was asking me questions about individual students. I told him the same thing I told the Vice Principal and I added that I have no idea as to the names of the kids, because it was the first time I was covering that room. I was asked repeatedly if I saw the laptop on the desk, and so on. They searched the room. They asked the students to open their backpacks. They had the students write down on paper - with their names and phone numbers - what they saw. They asked me to look through the teacher's desk, which I did, begrudgingly. Nothing came up. Soon, the class was over and I had a much needed break period; the police officer and Vice Principal left to sort out business.

It was during this break period that I heard the computer was found. I was sitting in the upstairs faculty room, reading my book, when I noticed the Vice Principal and some teachers were standing outside and discussing the incident. I snuck away from the table to get a good listen as to what they were saying. When they noticed me, they quieted down and departed. I asked the Vice Principal what happened, and she said they found it, and that everything's fine. That's it. She didn't say who did it, what happened, etc., just "everything's fine." It was as if I had no right to know at all, even though she was right on me not that long ago about what happened and how dare I be involved in any incident. That kind of indignation was so common in the District, it shouldn't have surprised me. I asked some of the other teachers what they knew - it bothered me enough to ask around - and all I could gather was that someone took the laptop, walked down the hallway, dropped it in another room out of the way and then went to class. It was a cheap, stupid, juvenile move, but these were cheap, stupid juvenile kids (in other schools, they would take the laptops of others and hide them in places - in closets, at the bottom of rectangular recycling bins - just to be silly).

It wasn't over, though. The next day, something else happened with that same exact class, with the same exact kid, Dodo. I had chewed them out for ruining my day, having me talk to the police, being accosted and questioned, and that I wasn't happy with it - on top of that, I was displeased with their changing seats and names on me, 'adopting' the names of others so that they could sit with their friends (they had assigned seats, but were going to do what they wanted to do - the class' "label," 7-A, denoted that they were a 'top-level' class of smarties). After a relatively easy going period and after getting through all the assignments they had in their textbook, there was less than five minutes left over. Now, I'm not sure what I said, but it was *something* to the effect of, "All right, we have less than five minutes left, so you can do what you want: you can read, do work from another class, work on projects on your laptops. You cannot move your seats." The class then went on doing what they had to do for that time before I told them they could leave to go to lunch. I thought everything was going well.

At the end of the day, the office called up to the room, looking for me and they wanted to see me before I left. Okay, I thought, no big deal. So I went down to the office, with my coat on and my lunch bag and book in hand. The secretary saw me and went to find the Principal, who ushered me into his office with his two Vice Principals in tow. Oh no, I thought. This is bad.

The Principal sat me down with his doltish lackeys and ran this by me: one of the students from 7-A, *that* class, was going on some sort of Sex Chat room and the students saw him doing it and reported it. I asked who the student was: it was Dodo, again, the same kid whose laptop was "stolen" the previous day, and his defense was priceless: that "the sub" (meaning me) "never said they *couldn't* play games in class" and that "they could do whatever they wanted." The Principal, and his silent toadies, sat silent while he asked me if I said that they *couldn't* play games on the computers. Now, I have no idea if I said that or not, but

I had said it in countless other schools: they can't play games on the computer unless the games they're playing are pre-approved and "educational." I told the Principal that I very well could have said they couldn't play games, but I was not positive. I was trying to be honest. Also, saying "they can do whatever they want," taken in loose context by me (meaning, do whatever schoolwork you want) was also challenged. I made the passive-aggressive comment that I don't remember everything I say and that no one can expect me to remember everything I say; if I do need to have everything I said repeated verbatim, next time I'll drag a court stenographer along with me. I was ushered out of the office after the Principal and the two Veeps gave each other knowing glances; I have no idea what the glances meant, but I felt angry at being interrogated, at being placed on equal footing as a teenager, when they could have done it covertly, talking to me on the sly, or just taking a firm stance with the kid, who knew, from the beginning of the year, that Sex Chat and games unapproved by the District are not allowed. But no, Fear ruled the day, and I was called before the Council.

In bringing me in the office, with Dodo standing outside the hallway - smirking at me, I recall - I was made to stand on equal footing with a 13-year-old, and by not taking the incident casually and immediately slamming down on the boy and me like a proto-tribunal, even having me sit in the same exact seat in the Principal's Office, spoke absolute volumes about how teachers - and the sub-teachers, like myself - are treated. I would have had no problem if I was privately asked what happened in class - the way it's happened in other schools - but the method of interrogation, calling me on the carpet, was cold and callous. My Mother's name was even dubiously invoked during the meeting with the Principal (and who the Principal knew full well) - after I said I could not recall every word I said, he pretended to pick up the phone, jokingly, and said, "Oh, I'm sure Mrs. Lotti should know her son can't remember what he said during the day." It was a frail attempt at humor and a thinly veiled cut at myself, as if *he*, as "superior" was threatening me, an "inferior," with calling *my* Mother!

For the record, I defiantly returned to that very school about a week later, and found out from a friend who works there that nothing happened to Dodo or the 7-A class for mischief. It should be noted that this Principal, in 2007, was caught trying to sell crystal meth *out of his office* and was arrested. At the time of his arrest, according to an article in the Morning Call, he was "naked and watching gay pornography with sex toys nearby." The article didn't include any comments from his mother, who must have been overjoyed by her son's accomplishments.

These arguments revolving around who-said-what have been frightening, and the incident with the Principal, Dodo and the two Veeps was not a unique one for me. I was reprimanded slightly by an Art Teacher at P— Elementary for using the word "Easter" when working on coloring projects - it was a Christian term, and forbidden in her room. In another art class, they couldn't work on Halloween projects because "Halloween" is a demonic holiday and "offends" some of the students who ascribe to religions that ban it. While reading a children's book at D— Elementary, someone in the hall overheard me, came into the room, pulled me aside and told me I should never read that book to the next couple of classes, because the book has the word "bomb" featured prominently in it and that the children are "sensitive" about the idea. Keep in mind, this was a classroom book and I did not bring it into the school.

It was a powerful lesson I learned: watch every single word that comes out of your mouth when teaching, in this fine, upstanding nation that claims to defend "free speech," but where speech isn't free at all. People are offended by this, offended by that. You can only say certain things to certain people, you cannot hold unacceptable beliefs that have not been pre-approved. The walls have ears.

7. Caught in the Funhouse Part III: Student Behavior in High School.

I sometimes preferred working in the High Schools to the other schools because it always seemed like I was given little to do and that the kids were more self-guided - as a sub, you hand them papers and they did them, and that was it. What I soon discovered was that you could hand papers to some classes and they would fill them out in relative silence, while others were full of difficult students who *really* didn't want to be in school and were going to challenge you every minute, and maybe even leave. Just … get up, and walk out.

I can certainly sympathize with the pressures of High School. The hormonal rage of Middle School carries over, and there's something very final about High School: the end of childhood, maybe, which is hard to face (but since some of them, coming from the backgrounds they did, never had a childhood, maybe that made it a lot tougher). Sure, college continues for some, but even that involves a separation from your parents and a heightened sense of responsibility (which sometimes doesn't always happen; I started college with more than a few people who never made it through). I understand crushes, since I had a few myself, and painful awkwardness. Saying High School is a microcosm of life is giving it a *lot* of credit, but there is a shred of truth to it.

Every instant I was in F— High School I kept scanning the classroom floor for likenesses between the kids in the seats and my own friends. It felt distant and a little frightening. Honestly, I was glad I didn't have to sit there anymore, worry about S.A.T.s and getting into college and maintaining my G.P.A., worrying if the girl I liked felt the same way, whether I looked nervous or awkward. Out of college and in my twenties, standing by the chalkboard and away from that former self, it was almost a relief: *that* was over, and I survived.

Yet, there were times when I looked upon those High School kids with utter confusion. Who *are* these people, I would say to myself. Since I went to Catholic School, there was a dress code that several people worked hard to break: one particular friend never wanted to wear his school sweater, so he often just slung it over his shoulder or carried it around like a dirty rag. You had to be clean-shaven, so if you had facial growth, you were given a razor. The girls fought the skirt-length mandate, rolling up the top to expose more leg, to entice the senses. I just wore whatever the hell they wanted me to wear, not bothering to be defiant: I realized that wearing a uniform doesn't necessarily change the person you are inside, it just changes your appearance. You can be an individual and not be absorbed into the void of conformity. Plus, I liked the idea of knowing what I was going to wear the next day.

Girls in public high schools were often seen walking around in their pajamas. Without getting graphic, one girl was wearing such a skimpy, button down pajama top - and no bra, evidently - that a portion of her breast was sticking out. Some could be seen with slippers. Some would carry around blankets. What happened to them? Nothing. The teachers were almost afraid to yell at them, and those that raised a fuss often got screamed at ("You're not my *goddamn parents*" one was overheard yelling). There was a dress code, sure, but it was barely enforced.

The boys in high school have a dress code, but it involves jackets and headwear: no long jackets (trench coats and the like - akin to the "Trench Coat Mafia" that blew away portions of Columbine), no hats, no hoods covering the head. Without a doubt, I saw kids wearing coats, wool caps pulled over disheveled hair, gold chains, long coats and so forth. Ah yes, defiance was in the air … but at least no one looked like they were ready for sleepy time.

Disgusting behavior, however, knew no bounds. A custodian informed me that one of the students actually defecated behind the stairwell leading to the second floor of the building. It's not uncommon for whole trays of uneaten food to get dumped on the floor and left there. A former friend of mine - and I use the term "friend" loosely - had a habit of spitting his "dip" all over the floor instead of in a juice jar, leaving it for someone else to tend to. Perhaps this is in preparation for dorm living in college, where in some of the bathrooms, if there's no toilet paper, students would use the shower curtain to clean their posterior, or in the dorm rooms themselves, where rats and rodents become problems because unused food was not disposed of, but rather "stuffed" into corners (or desk drawers).

Now, of both local High Schools, I spent one and only one day at one of them, L— High, but had such an awful experience I swore I would never return. I've spoken with some people who like L— High School over F— High School because the kids at L— High School are "less snooty," but I'll take snooty over barbaric, pretentious over slovenly. Maybe it was my upbringing.

I was covering a Junior (11th grade at L— High School) English class for a young female teacher who had a seminar to attend to - she set everything out for me to do and explained it, which was certainly nice: it's much more accommodating than me showing up and not knowing where everything is and spending the first fifteen minutes hurriedly sifting through paperwork while students start to pile into the classroom. The local High Schools were set up in four 'block' segments - with time given for lunch -

and most teachers I knew of only taught for three of those blocks, leaving one of them for Preparation Time or a Team Meeting or something along those lines. For this woman, her last block was the Prep period, so that was supposed to mean I had nothing to do that period (I couldn't leave the building, but I could read or have a snack). Believe me: one anticipates a Prep Period the way one anticipates sex on the second date. You watch the clock and pray for it to happen.

The first three periods weren't intolerable, but they were noisy and resistant to doing work - they had to read a play and act out the parts, but resisted volunteering and the class grinded to a halt, leaving me to read the play and hand out the paperwork (which the teacher wanted me to collect and grade). Most refused to do the paperwork and a lot of them drew over the papers, so I collected the disfigured paperwork. Hey, it wasn't my grade.

Around the end of the third period, a wonderful thing happened. The Assistant Principal called me up on the phone I tried using earlier but couldn't dial out, saying he needed me to fill in for a class for the Prep Period whose teacher needed to attend some kind of student hearing and would only take "about fifteen minutes." I wasn't happy, but I had no choice: I figured, what's fifteen minutes? I could live with that. So once the fourth block came up, I was waiting for the next teacher to bring his students to the class.

He arrived right on time, carrying with him a video and a stack of worksheets. He told me that the class should watch the video, when it was over, do the worksheet and while doing the worksheet, I was to write notes on the board for them to copy down in their notebooks. It sounded easy, and since it was only going to take fifteen minutes, hey, no problem.

Something struck me as the class came in, yelling and pushing each other: this was not an ordinary group. Most of them looked like they stepped out of a rap video, with chains and long coats and hoods pulled over their heads. The regular teacher yelled back at a few of them to shut up and sit down, told them he was going to a meeting, that he'd be back and told them what work they were going to do. The class didn't listen and he, resigned, just took his satchel and left. Before walking out the door, he stressed that no one was to leave. I nodded and he left.

I put the video on, turned out the lights and stood in the back of the classroom. I don't remember what the name of the movie was, but it was violent, and Natives were using spears to kill each other. The class cheered the murders and bloodshed. But in less than five minutes, it was over, credits rolling, and I turned the lights back on. In one corner the one kid was throwing coins at the girl sitting two seats down from him, and I told him to stop. He kept going, so I moved him to the back of the class. When I started handing out worksheets, I saw him take his things and leave the room. I asked the class where he went, and they told me he was leaving and that he wasn't allowed to leave. I went to the back of the room, but he was gone. I picked up the phone and tried to dial the office, but it kept ringing (I suspected something was wrong with the phone, but was told later on it was 'fine,' which I think is ridiculous).

The class was getting rowdy, saying that I was going to get fired for him leaving the room. I told them I didn't care, that they should work on the worksheets, and that I had to write something on the board, and to get quiet, and all those other things. I kept one eye on the clock to check when exactly this guy was going to come back - it was close to fifteen minutes, but he was nowhere to be seen. When I turned around to write the notes on the board, someone threw a coin at me, hitting me in the shirt. I turned back and one of the girls said she needed to go to the bathroom. I told her she could go. She went with another girl, and when the two left, one of the boys in the class told me that they couldn't go together, so he ran out of the room, too.

When I walked to the back to yell at all of them in the hallway, no one was there; upon returning to the room, half the class was walking around the room and switching seats. I kept looking at the clock, hoping the regular teacher would return soon. I gave one of the girls in the class the chalk to write on the board since I didn't want to turn my back on the class. As I made my way over to the desk, someone threw a sandwich at me - yes, a sandwich - which splattered on the wall. One of the kids ran up by me and picked the sandwich up off the ground, yelling that so-and-so (another boy in the room) threw *his* sandwich, so he picked the tomato and lettuce off the wall, 'rebuilt' his meal, went back to his seat, and ate it. One of the boys raised his hand to go to the bathroom, and when I said too many people had left the room already, he said he was going to 'shit his pants.' Resigned, I told him to go. I looked at the clock again: a half-hour was gone.

One of the remaining boys in the class took one of the girls' backpacks and opened the door and chucked it into the hallway. I thought, this was enough, so I wandered out into the hallway and told the next door teacher that I was having a problem, and asked if he could talk to the class and calm them down. He told me he was busy, but he'd stop over "in time." Those were his words: "In time."

I went back in, and the rest of the kids remaining in class were still wandering around the room. I sat down at the desk and stuffed pieces of tissue into my ears and glanced up everyone once in a while to make sure coins or sandwiches weren't flying at my face. I no longer cared what they did, or who knew about it. I must have been lost in whatever it was I was doing, and the tissues plugged in my ears must have been working, because the lights flickered and a police officer was standing in the back of the room. He had a young man with a black hooded sweatshirt in front of him. The police officer asked, "Is he in this class?" I told the officer I didn't know, but the kids in the class were laughing, saying, "Yeah, yeah, he's in here." The police officer left and shut the door. The young man came into the room, sat on the desk and said to me, "Hey, Mister, what the fuck I gotta do?" I laughed at this (which I shouldn't have, but it was so bluntly put) and told him to just wait for the regular teacher to show up. He said, "Nah, I'm leaving," got up, and left the room again.

I was puzzled and chuckling out of frustration and desperation - what else was I to do? The one girl in the front of the class said to me, "He's not in this class," and I shook my head. Two of the girls who left earlier came back into the room asking me if I saw a cop in the hallway. I told them I did. The two of them told me that the kid with the black hooded sweatshirt had *tackled* two *other* girls on the second floor of the building (the class I was covering was on the third floor), ripped their student identification badges off them (*ripped* off, they said), ran into the boy's bathroom with the badges and was taunting the girls to come in and get them. The girls ran to the school police officer to get their badges back. The young man with the badges, these two girls were telling me, had locked himself in one of the stalls, and the officer had to talk him out of there. I asked the girls how they knew this, and they said it's because they were in the hallway watching it happen with everyone else.

I was trying to make sense of this: you mean the police officer, who found out that the girls were *tackled* by this rogue, didn't bother taking the kid away, or pressing charges or anything like that, he just ... *sent* the kid back to a room, any room, just to get rid of him? And the room *I* was in no less, a room he didn't even belong in? Amazing.

More time passed. I tried not paying attention to them, aimlessly flipping through a book and clockwatching. One of the remaining boys in the room raised his hand and asked to go to the bathroom. I told him, no way, I don't want anything like the police officer thing happening again, I don't want to see any more cops. He then, and this is the most priceless, the most vile thing of all: he went to the back of the room, pulled down his pants and urinated into the garbage can. The few kids left in the class got hysterical, and I became frozen. He finished, walked over to his desk, got his backpack and left.

I told the rest of the class, if you want to leave, leave, I don't care any more. Some stayed and read their books, but the rest of the class took their things and ran for the exit, pushing and shoving their way out the door. The dismissal bell rang about twenty minutes later, the regular teacher who said he would come back never did, and I just got my coat, my things and left the room in the disheveled state it was in. *Screw them*, I thought.

I went straight to the office and asked them about where the teacher was, and why he didn't come back. I relayed the story, and the secretaries told me that was "strange," because the meeting only lasted fifteen minutes. I'm not sure who was telling the truth, but the reality of it was grim: I was left with the equivalent of an out-of-control mentally disturbed class with work they wouldn't do. It wasn't simply stressful, it was dangerous.

This particular school, L— High School, has been known for its problems. As I've said before, none of this is in the inner city where you'd "expect" it, but they acted like delinquents. I was told by another substitute that she wouldn't go there because she witnessed, one day, during a Pep Rally for the football team in the auditorium, the kids were passing around a baby like a beach ball - it seems that baby's mother didn't want to miss the Pep Rally, didn't 'drop off' the child at the day care center built into the school, had brought it to the auditorium, and was just passing it around to the other students. I was not there so I did not see this personally, but if she was trying to one-up my story about the kid urinating in the garbage can, it's pretty close. I'm sure everyone who has worked at that place for a long time - and isn't in a padded cell being fed medication 24 hours a day - has plenty to tell.

The High School is also no stranger to drug use, either. I've heard countless 'rumors' and very brief anecdotes from other teachers, but one true-life incident was well-publicized in the local papers. In October of the 2004-2005 school year, there was an incident where some students that were already at school *left* the school early in the morning to pick up friends. With four people in the car, the driver got into an accident, failing to stop at a stop sign and running into a (mercifully empty) school bus, killing one of her friends in the car and seriously injuring the other two. The female driver, who was sixteen at the time, pled guilty to vehicular homicide and, here's the real cause of the accident: she was under the influence of a controlled substance, marijuana. In another case, a sixteen year old former football player from the same school was found dead in New York City in a drug-related turf war. Later, a young girl at the same school was killed by her boyfriend and her body was thrown off to the side of a random road. I saw the shrine made up by friends, with T-shirts and banners and crosses adorning the nearby fence. In 2015, a kid was busted at that same school for $4k worth of cocaine and heroin. You don't need to watch *The Wire* when it's happening in your neighborhood.

8. Waking Up To Harassment.

The pressures to conform and be popular are timeless, but today it seems as if the abused aren't taking it so easily, often lashing out in extreme violence, as was made so very famous in the numerous school shootings and bomb threats around the United States. I've never noticed it in Elementary Schools, where if the students don't like someone in particular they *more or less* ignore them or don't want them in their group or don't pick them for gym or things like that, while in Middle School they taunt and badger and harass and in High School they physically abuse, taunt, spread rumors and make life a living hell.

In one Middle School a group of girls were picking on another girl sitting a few seats down from them. I'd already moved around the group of girls, trying to stop them from bothering the other girl, but it wasn't successful. No matter where I placed them in the room, they would still yell things. This was a major distraction, and soon the whole class, like scared jackals, all teamed up with the girls to pick on the lone girl, who just wanted to be left alone. Eventually, she grew sick of being harassed, and said something to the one girl a few desks down from her. I have no idea what it pertained to - the fighting started well before this particular class - but it enraged the other girl so much she lunged over the desks between them, crawling over the boys sitting between them, and smacked the girl right in the face. The oppressed girl smacked her back - lightly, ineffectually - and then the other girl started hitting harder. I yelled, ran over and did my best to get my arms between them. I sent them both to the Guidance Counselor along with escorts at different times so they wouldn't fight in the hallways.

Another occasion, at B— Middle School, two students - about 13 or 14 - came in the classroom and were arguing a little bit. The boy said something to the girl, and then the girl called the boy a curse word, and the boy, not at all pleased with being "disrespected," grabbed her hair, pulled her towards him, slapped her in the face and said, "Don't you ever speak to me in that tone again." It was like something I saw in a movie. I intervened, the boy apologized, but the girl wouldn't stop crying. I told the girl to go to the bathroom to wash up, but she never came back to class. The boy sat there the rest of the class looking infuriated. The great relief was that I didn't have to give a testimonial later as to what happened - sadly, more and more, I just got sick of being called out on the carpet for things the students said or did to each other and was grateful for having others to deal with the countless problems.

When I asked an Assistant Principal sometime after that what he recommended I do in cases where students were fighting - I don't recall how I got enmeshed in a discussion about it, but I do know it wasn't a conversation I started - he said the best thing to do was let them "beat each other until they get tired" then "call security." I asked him why not intervene, and he said that he worked at another Middle School where one woman got in the middle and was cut with the knife of one of the combatants. "It's not worth it," he said. I was told by my Godmother, who worked for years as a cafeteria worker in a Middle School, that one of the teachers there tried to stop a fight and wound up with a dislocated shoulder from one of the kids who grabbed her arm and yanked it out of the socket.

A few of the students from F— High School told me a story about one classroom with large windows that extended to the ground and faced the courtyard. One afternoon, a student outside the building saw someone in seated in a class that he was having an dispute with (over what isn't entirely the point), took a brick or large rock from outside of the school (where he got it from no one knew), smashed the large window, grabbed the student out of the classroom, dragged him *outside* the building over the broken glass and proceeded to beat him senseless, putting the other boy into the hospital. One of the kids that was telling me the story was in the class at the time it happened, and said that everyone in the room - including the teacher - sat there stunned and paralyzed, forced to look in fear and horror at the unexpected window shattering and violence to happen in the middle of what was an ordinary class.

In a weird way, it makes me feel a little more comfortable to know that I'm not the only one who's felt powerless to stop fighting, harassment or violence. At L— High School, they had a swimming pool where the students played water polo. The substitute I spoke to told me that, as a woman covering boy's gym, she didn't think it was the wisest of lesson plans for the regular gym teacher to leave - she was wearing a business suit (this particular woman was always dressed well), and she wasn't about to stand very close to the water because of the splashing. Taking full advantage of this, the one class, picking on one of the weaker boys in the room, were trying to drown him using the floating box that was supposed to be a goal, putting it on top of his head and collectively pushing down. After she pleaded with them to let him alone, she found someone to come over and put an end to it.

That kind of helplessness was really all-encompassing, and even I became a target with some of the less-stable members of E— Middle School, who started calling me the "faggot substitute" and wouldn't stop. I told another teacher about it, Mr. Walrus, but Mr. Walrus was, as I found out later, a "friend" of the kids (one of those teachers stuck in a time warp, trying to be their 'pal' but shirking his essentially parental responsibilities), and did nothing to stop them. Every time I wandered into the 8th grade wing, I would hear someone call me some slur, and I had to just ignore them. If their own teachers wouldn't put an end to the taunts, what else could I do?

I have to admit, by being taunted myself by the rude and homophobic students, I actually got a miniscule taste of what Dylan Klebold and Eric Harris of Columbine High School, Colorado felt when they were mocked in similar ways. It really is a horrible feeling. Every time I would see the main students, the key rabble rousers, who called me "Mr. Maricon" and things like that, I felt hate and disgust and how it would be so much better for those people to not be around me or near me, how it would make my day more pleasant. I admit that I've already asked the Sub Caller Batty to move me to different rooms on days I was booked ahead of time, just so I could avoid those kids. It's not that I was scared of them, I just didn't want to be picked on and be left alone. Hell, I wasn't even picked on like that when I was in high school.

So as I was the target of mockery - as an adult - I was also helpless as a person to stop those being mocked, like the fat girl in the one Middle School who was wearing clothes too small for her so that her obese flesh stuck out of the bottom of her shirt, to the mock-horror of her classmates who would hit her on the head as they passed, or the boys who would steal from one another and I had to tell them to give the item back to them, or the small young lad who was standing in line for lunch and got punched in the back of the head for not getting out of another kid's way (I saw the whole thing since I had lunch duty that particular day). I couldn't stop the slaps, the torment, the name-calling, and neither could (or maybe even would) the other teachers. You can tell a bunch of young toughs to "knock it off" only so much; they stop hearing you after a little bit, and then get even when they're out in the hallway.

It wouldn't be out of line to state that the problem with kids being beat up in school for being different has been around since the beginning of schooling. The problem is that the level of violence is escalating, and that teachers are even being threatened. I was told by the mother of a boy at one Middle School that some of the members of the football team - who were written up by one teacher for misbehavior and then couldn't participate in the football game on Friday (horrors!) - slashed the tires of the offending teacher. At N— Middle School, a fourteen-year-old (on March 2, 2005) was charged with "aggravated assault; pushed and cursed at a teacher" (the case was referred to Northampton County Juvenile Probation). At S— Elementary School, one of the teachers' laptops was stolen and never recovered. At D— Elementary School, one of the teachers' laptops was stolen *and sold*. (No one ever stole anything from me - I always brought with me a coffee mug filled with hot tea, a bag with a sandwich and fruit in it and a book. That's it. A cell phone or laptop were always prime pickings - my paperback copy of *Exile and the Kingdom* was always perfectly safe.)

It would be terribly naïve to think that incidents of threats and beatings are confined to school grounds. An incident that started between two 5th grade girls - yes, girls - in their neighborhood had carried over after school. One of the girls, who had a 'cousin' at the Middle School and was 13, brought the cousin with her to the other girl's house, got the girl out of her house and the two of them beat her up so badly that the victim was put in the hospital. I was told this by the mother of a friend of the victimized girl, who was in the same class. It's been since "quieted up" by the school - the 5th grade girl who was the attacker mysteriously went "to Florida" and the other one was apparently kicked out of Middle School, though this hasn't been confirmed. (This is in line with the articles I've been reading about increasing violence among young females by the F.B.I.)

If the police, the teachers, *anyone* cannot properly punish someone for an obvious crime, where's the deterrent? You mean to tell me that now Elementary Schools are going to start becoming target zones? What's going to stop a 1st grader from wielding a pair of scissors like a knife and threatening to stab her teacher in the hand for giving her a failing grade on a spelling test? Oh wait, that actually happened, at R— Elementary School, 1st grade, late 2005. At least the little girl was expelled.

9. Murder Insurance!

— A crime occurs on school grounds every six seconds, making it approximately 3 million a year. (National Education Association)

— 1 in 20 High School students has reported taking a gun to school. (National Education Association)

When one of the Correctional Officers from the local prison showed up to do a "program" for some of the problem students in one of the Middle Schools I was covering, I wrote down on a piece of paper those two statistics he had shown on a PowerPoint presentation. After the talk, I asked him about those numbers, which seemed to me to be outrageous, where he got them from ("They're well known," is all he said) and his thoughts on violence in schools. He seemed rather sick of it all, and the basis of his message was: society is becoming less civil, and there's no disputing it.

Following these two grizzly points (the man did not have precise research, so there's no telling which particular years the two statistics were referring to ... he probably invented them over a coffee break), the question remains: what solutions have our think-tanks manufactured for the protection of our teachers and students and staff from violence? Metal detectors are a great idea but certainly avoidable - take a look at the 2005 Red Lake Massacre, in which gunman Jeffrey Weise *drove over* them and then proceeded into the school and on with his rampage. Our district never even bothered to install these devices, which while not perfect, might have provided a slight peace of mind. Perhaps they were too busy spending money on buying those laptops as a part of the aforementioned Skill-21 program.

Since teachers' hands are tied in terms of punishing students - no physical contact, no 'unfair' yelling (read: discrimination) - perhaps teachers should seriously consider the miracle of *Murder Insurance*, offered by the National Education Association, which is a policy that protects teachers "if death is caused by an unlawful homicide which occurs while the eligible member is engaged in any activity which is in the express or implied terms of an eligible member's occupation" - that is, if the teacher in question is murdered while in the classroom or on a field-trip. So look on the bright side, instructors: if you're dead, at least your family is provided for.

The National Rifle Association, as reported by Arthur Rotstein of the Associated Press (March 25, 2005), has apparently advocated some guns for some teachers as a 'solution' to the question of safety and defense. Notice the word 'some.' According to vice-president Sandra S. Froman:

"I'm not saying that that means every teacher should have a gun or not, but what I am saying is we need to look at all the options at what will truly protect the students ... No gun law, no policy that you could implement now or that was already implemented, I think, could possibly prevent someone so intent on destruction. I think everything's on the table as far as looking at what we need to do to make our schools safe for our students."

Froman cited the school shooting in Mississippi back in 1997 when the then 16-year-old attacker Luke Woodham was held at bay by a male teacher who retrieved a gun out of his car. The local middle and high schools all have armed police officers - some regularly patrol the buildings, but others just seem to hide in their offices. In other words, there *was* someone in the schools I was at that had a weapon ... but is the NRA suggesting that the one police officer with the one pistol isn't enough? Who designates the teachers who are to be armed (this "discussion" was brought up - again - after the Sandy Hook Elementary School attack in 2012 and the Stoneman Douglas High School shooting in 2018)? Plus, wouldn't it be equally dangerous placing a weapon in the vicinity of a potentially stressed-out and/or depressed teacher, considering the high turnover rate in the profession?

Corporal punishment doesn't appear to be a logical choice, taking it upon the stressed teacher to wail upon the child. Never mind that some people that went to Catholic school in the past and were often hit by nuns and priests with rulers or openly humiliated grew up to be sane and productive. My Father told me the Sisters used to smack their knuckles; my late Grandfather told me they used to paddle him and his classmates for bad behavior; my Mother's one teacher called up my Grandmother to complain that my Mother was "swinging her feet too much under her desk" (if you can believe it); I was made to stand in the corner holding Math books in both hands for failing a basic arithmetic test. A famous saying, "Spare the rod and spoil the child" exists for a reason, but placing the rod in the teacher's hand instead of the parent's might be ill-advised.

An article in 2000 by Paul Wiseman of the *USA Today* illustrated the problem with giving permission to teachers to physically punish: In China, a 4th grade math teacher told 28 boys to beat up a classmate who didn't do his homework, who then ended up in the hospital (the article stated that the attack may have lasted some 40 minutes). A psychology professor from the University of Hong Kong, David Ho, was cited as saying that, "It's really very deeply rooted in the cultural tradition, the idea of public

76

humiliation as a way to teach people to conform." This is exactly the kind of excess that doesn't solve anything.

There certainly has to be some intermediary step - some gray area between the Fear of the Students which prevails and the more extreme Humiliation and Physical Abuse. Some of those suggested by experts don't always work. For example, stern warnings and isolation (moving kids away from the rest of the class) often makes them only want to be noticed more - and naturally, if they're making noise in the back of the room, the other kids will most likely keep turning around to see whatever he/she is doing next. One student I placed in the back of the room at a Middle School "disappeared" after he got tired of yelling - when I wandered to the back of the room to see what happened, I found that he was lying on the floor, "asleep."

The existence of school psychologists is also supposed to help them with their interpersonal problems - after heated arguments or some fights, the students are sent to the guidance office to 'talk things out.' Speaking as someone with a degree in Psych (whatever that's worth nowadays), I do believe it works to a certain degree, so this isn't a bad thing, to me, and the guidance office acting as an intermediary in arguments is better than the teenagers settling it themselves. Some of the kids are smart, however - they leave the guidance office, go outside and fight out there (sometimes it boils over back in the classroom, where another pointless tiff re-ignites the conflict). Let's not even bother with the problem of gangs in schools and rivalries and whatnot - though they exist, I would have had no idea who was in what gang. I was told they recruit them young, however, by promising enticing things, like game consoles or good old cash.

There's an 'in-school' suspension program set up in our District referred to as CA/MP (or, Character, Academic, and Motivation Program) but I was told by the students that went there that it was "better than real school." When I asked them to clarify, they said they were given less work than in their regular classes, watched videos on respecting others, talked about things that bothered them or "did worksheets." Having never been there myself, it's difficult to say whether or not they were blowing me off with a lazy description and it was genuinely awful or whether it was indeed a weak punishment for errant behavior. If the kids are right, however, it sounds just like hokum.

One Middle School I went to realized there was a problem and set up a system to address it. If you were having any trouble with a class, or with a student in the class, you gave them three warnings, then dialed '3333' and told the secretary you're having a problem in whatever room. The Vice-Principal - a no-nonsense character - would come up, you would tell him who the offenders were, and he would write their names down for a two-hour detention. Few questions were asked - all you had to do was point out the offenders (in order words, they expected problems). If the detentions added up, students received the dreaded Saturday detention, which was enforced. No one - and I mean *no one* - wants a Saturday detention. Don't get me wrong - none of this works particularly well: attendance among students is still poor (they show up late because their alarm clocks go off late or their parents, seemingly without jobs of their own, neglect to wake them) and the school has countless disciplinary problems. But for me, at least, it was a school I never felt like I'd have a serious problem with: it was a school that took a lot of troubled kids from bad backgrounds. People warned me off going there - "They'll tear you apart" - but the one thing I liked about it, like the Elementary Schools from the same neighborhoods that fed into it - was that I'd get backing from the others, which was all I asked for. Their heads weren't in the sand - there were going to be issues, and I wasn't going to be blamed. Granted, even with that support it was hard to tolerate class after class of defiance, but it was never boring, and I never drove home thinking, "I'm going to get in trouble over that one class that was fighting or screaming."

The other middle and High Schools weren't so 'aware' of the problems or all that staunch in keeping a stiff back. Some didn't even bother giving out detentions or writing up "Code of Conduct" forms regarding infractions. I was 'fortunate' enough to have students from a class I had a problem with - and wrote their names down on the sub form for their teacher to be aware that they were problems for me - in another, smaller class, and I asked them what their regular teacher did to them as 'punishment,' if anything. They told me that the teacher didn't give them detention, but instead gave them 'extra homework.' Extra homework. These two boys were doing cartwheels in the back of the class - one kicked a girl in the shoulder - and I sent them both out of the room (and documented the occurrence in relative detail), and they got 'extra homework?' That's ... that's just more work that they won't do when they get home! Why not bake them cookies and really torture them? I took this up with a teacher friend who worked in the building - we started subbing around the same time; she got a full-time job the following year - and she admitted that detentions were 'punishment' for the teachers, and since a lot of them had after-school jobs, courses for their Master's Degree, doctor's appointments, coaching jobs, etc., it was an undue hardship on them.

It's certainly true that B— Middle School's strong detention policy wasn't exactly a deterrent to uncooperative behavior, so maybe the teachers at E— Middle School were correct in not being vehement in defending it, realizing they're actually detaining themselves, not engaging in behavior modification. I know from personal experience that the phone call home was always something *I* dreaded, but that was because my parents never took my side - only my teacher's - because they were actually *parents*, and taking the word of an *adult* over that of a *child* was *sensible* (in most cases). Often times, when I've sat in the Faculty Room (which I tried never to do, but it was inevitable in middle and High Schools where every classroom was needed, and where during prep time I had no place left to sit down and drink my coffee), there was always some teacher on the telephone, calling up parents. For convenience, the students' contact information was always left beside the phone either in an alphabetized binder or on index cards. I would pretend to read the local paper and often listen in on the conversations - it was usually something to the extent of "Your son/daughter did not do the project that was due for X number of weeks and is failing my class" or "Your son/daughter was misbehaving in class in the following ways..." and then listing them. When I pried and asked the teachers what the parents would say in response, the teachers would typically tell me they were paid lip-service, making countless excuses like "We were away for the weekend" and "He's been stressed out lately." Sometimes the parents would say, "I'll get on him/her, he/she will straighten up," which is what the teacher wanted to hear. Since I couldn't do my own follow-up and check in later to see if the student did straighten up, it's anyone's guess if the phone call did any good.

Some of the times, however, the teacher making the phone calls - and there were a lot of prep time phone calls, at least in my experience - would get frustrated because none of the numbers he/she tried were answered - including private cell phone numbers (e-mails bounced back or were never replied to). In other words, the parent was, in all likelihood, screening calls (or deleting messages). He/she would leave a very polite message stating the problem, then ask to be called back at school or even at home. Sometimes if there was a major issue, the parent would get called at work. When I'd ask if talking to the parents helped in dealing with the students, most I spoke to said something to the effect of, "I'm just doing my own due diligence."

10. To Nurture and Neglect.

To take even the most furtive of glances at the statistics related to maltreatment in the American family is absolutely unsettling. To do actual research on the topic is even more unnerving. Listed below are but a few that I found to be of particular interest:

— Each day in the United States, more than 3 children die as a result of child abuse in the home. Most of the children who die are younger than six years of age. (U.S. Department of Health and Human Services, Administration on Children, Youth and Families, Child Maltreatment 2001, Washington, DC: U.S. Government Printing Office, 2003)

— The rate of infant homicide reached a 30-year high in 2000. (from "Infant Homicide," a report issued December 2002 by Child Trends, an independent research organization)

— Child abuse is reported - on average - every 10 seconds. (U.S. Department of Health and Human Services, Administration on Children, Youth and Families, Child Maltreatment 2001, Washington, D.C.: U.S. Government Printing Office, 2003)

— One of every seven victims of sexual assault reported to law enforcement agencies were under age six. Frequently, the person who sexually molests a child is also a child. (From the National Incident-Based Reporting

System. Data based on reports from law enforcement agencies for years 1991 through 1996, U.S. Department of Justice.).

— Nearly one-half of substantiated cases of child neglect and abuse are associated with parental alcohol or drug abuse. (Child Welfare League of America: Alcohol and Other Drug Survey of State Child Welfare Agencies. Washington, D.C.: Child Welfare League of America, 1997).

If the child's home life is not going to be a place of comfort and security - as it clearly isn't in these chosen statistics, what kind of mental state does anyone expect them to be in once they come to school? While not all children that are abused show visual signs of it like bruising, scars, sores, and so on, how many of them are resilient enough to deal with that, come to class and be able to concentrate properly?

As for myself, if a student would try telling me about what happened at home, I would stop them and tell them to talk to their regular teacher or guidance counselor about it. Why the distance? First off, I was afraid of being interrogated by the *other teachers* for being nosy with the students and their personal lives. Their personal lives should stay at home, as should mine. There was no room for one-to-one talk - I was clearly not a counselor. Second, I didn't *want* to hear their stories. I made the mistake of asking a girl who was about 9-years-old - who sat out the gym class I was covering - why her leg was in a cast and if it was skiing or from a car accident. She told me she "tripped over her Dad's beer can and fell down the steps." I didn't buy this response one instant but didn't pursue it. It was none of my business.

It was also none of my business to delve into the lives of the other students who would act out, give me a hard time, or give the other students a hard time. At some point - around my third year of teaching - I started doing a little sleuth-work of my own to figure out who to "look out for" (since the classroom teacher rarely told me): I would scan the class roster sheets and check the students' personal information, which had listed their Social Security Numbers, home addresses, phone numbers and so on. Nine out of ten times, the student that gave me problems had only *one* parent listed under "Parents/Contacts." One. I'm not saying it would be out of the ordinary for said student to have two parents, because there were times where the wild one had two parents.   This is not scientifically measured or anything like that, but I found it to be a fairly reliable indicator for myself, at least - it gave me a heads up as to who in the room could be a potential day-ruiner. It wasn't always 100% - I'd say more along the lines of 60-65%, but that's as good an alert system as I was going to have. As for the entire classes that were out of control, I stood alone against all, and aside from walking them down to the office, dropping them off and saying "You deal with them" and getting in my car, I just had to put up with them. This brings to mind one morning at D— Elementary. I was called in to cover for a Learning Support class, but the door was locked. I asked the secretary if the custodian could open it for me. The two of us walked down the hallway and we came up to two adjacent doors. He unlocked one, asked me what teacher I was in for and after I told him, he closed that door and said, "Sorry, that's the room for the gifted kids.   You're in the class next door with the worthless ones."

Regarding the students' physical appearance, some would come in with dirty clothes, food stains on their faces, holes in the knees of their jeans. I wouldn't be surprised if some of them wore the same things every day. One girl, at L— Elementary, was complaining of an ear-ache. The teacher sent her to the nurse to get checked. She couldn't see anything at first, but when she looked closer she found that there was a tic lodged in the girl's ear. That's nothing - at a relatively nice school, G— Elementary, a boy came in with *fleas*. The teachers that came into contact with him - as well as teacher assistants (the boy was in Learning Support, so he was struggling in school), were scratching themselves all day. The boy wasn't in my class, but I was in the building that day. I went home and immediately threw all my clothes in the wash and rinsed off my hair.

At S— Elementary, another generally agreeable school and one of the schools I usually liked going to, I was wandering around the top floor during my break period to get a cup of coffee and use the restroom. The top floor had this horrific odor to it, and when I got into the faculty room, the regular teachers were also complaining about where the smell was coming from. After some investigation, they found the culprit: one of the boys in the 4th grade, and specifically, his backpack. As it turns out, the smell was cat urine, and the cause was that the boy's backpack doubled as the cat's house to sleep in and (apparently) deposit waste. The boy was sent home to get cleaned up, but the smell lingered in the hallway until the end of the day.

These children clearly came from homes in which their cleanliness was neglected. So many of them come to school from homes that are less than ideal. Neglect is easy to see, but something like sexual abuse is private and shameful. The above statistic notes that most often the individual that molests a child is often a child, maybe a slightly older brother or sister or neighbor; in Tim Roth's film *The War Zone*, it was the father - played brilliantly by the great Ray Winstone - that was molesting the children. I met so many children that were disturbed it was, without actually speaking to them on a one-to-one basis, impossible to know what the disturbance was caused by, so I cannot claim to know how common the problem is based on stories told to me. Several Elementary School students have gotten in trouble for making crude drawings of people engaging in sexual acts, though whether this is a simple process of 'copying' what they see on TV, a movie or the Internet or even their home life is unclear.

Therefore, it's purely physical evidence that I can vouch for and attest to. I was astonished, for example, to find out that the largest local Middle School, E— Middle School, had a "Breakfast Pass" program wherein the students, instead of reporting to homeroom, would go to the cafeteria and get a tray full of quasi-nutritious breakfast things - bagels and toast and cereal. I had to cover this a few times when I was in for the same teacher throughout the year, and got nosy about the program so I was asking around as to how and why the students "qualify" for it. Supposedly it was set up for the children from homes in which their parents couldn't or wouldn't wake up in the morning to make them food before they went to school, so the school once more had to act as a surrogate parent and feed the children. This was not for one or two kids, mind you - the morning Breakfast Pass students were often close to one hundred or even two hundred, although I never took an official tally.

To me, it's unfathomable: the parents couldn't even give them a bowl of cereal to eat and some juice! In some of the Elementary Schools from lower-income families, the food was brought *to* the homeroom - the kids would get, say, a muffin and a small pint of milk. Sometimes a muffin or two was left over from students that were absent, and the kids would push each other out of the way for it - I usually tried to take a poll of how many kids in the class wanted the extra muffin(s) and divided the remaining food into sections, giving everyone a little more. I thought of creating a trivia game to see who could "win" the extra food, but it just seemed cruel.

Some of the kids in high school that 'qualify' for a free lunch - they come from such poor backgrounds - often, out of pride, *refuse* to partake in it, so ashamed of being given a free lunch when the other kids have to pay for it. It goes along with the territory, though, and makes perfect sense. I had a conversation with one of the teachers in one of the High Schools about this and she mentioned to me that she thought the schools should probably stay open until 5 PM (a sort of 'High School Day Care'), and serve dinner for the kids, since they're probably not getting that at home, either. She mused that they could even run a special program from school closing time (3:00 for middle, 2:30 for high) to 5 PM where students that wanted/needed extra help could get it, but then dismissed her flight of fancy, saying that (a.) no one would stay (teachers or students) and that it (b.) simply wasn't in the budget. Isn't a 7 hr. school day long enough, anyway? If they don't learn in that period of time, day after day, are they ever going to?

Naturally, the 'opposite' end of that would be the 'over-involved' parents, the ones who call repeatedly and harass the Principals and teachers, the ones who stand behind their children 1,000% even when the child is wrong. I'm not saying parents shouldn't support their kids, but there's a fanaticism to some that causes riptides of problems internally, making everyone's job more difficult. By not backing the teacher and administration - as *adults* - and defending a child who, in any particular instance, could be wrong or lying, this suggests to the child that he/she is above the system at all times, able to get away with anything. Some of the 'better' schools have nothing but over-involved parents who come down on the Principals and then, during school hours, the Principals come down on the teachers. I was told, by a woman who used to teach 5th grade at one of the Elementary Schools and had since asked to be removed from one of these schools fraught with over-involved parents, that she had a friend who taught at one of the local private academies and who said that if you looked at a student the wrong way you were guaranteed to hear about it later (it's an exaggeration, of course, but I'm sure she means that students come home with complaints about their teachers all the time and the way they feel they should be treated). One of the teachers at a Middle School told me that he just wanted to go to a district where, on parent's night, the parents came up to him and said, "If my son/daughter gives you a hard time, call me. The next day he/she will have a *completely different attitude.*" I told this teacher that my father was exactly the same way - parents of that *demeanor*, the tough-but-fair mold, were all too rare. You try avoiding the extremes of the neglectful parents and the over-involved parents and start searching for that all-elusive middle ground where teachers can actually do their jobs without fear.

To play fair for the parents, it isn't easy being a disciplinarian these days. Yes, there are those parents that give in too easily, placing their little precious ones on a throne of ignorance, and there are the parents who are chronically abusive, hurting the future of the society on a deep emotional and physical level. But what about those that actually try to discipline their kids? When scolding stops working and taking away privileges becomes tired and routine, what else can you do? Physical punishment has been rendered outdated in the 21st century, where the new fad appears to be that of "children calling the police on their parents." I've heard of instances from teachers and parents I've spoken with about parents that threaten punishment on their children for misbehavior only for their very own children to run to their friends' houses and call the police *on them.* The kicker isn't that the police laugh off the phone call, but that the police actually police the family, and arrest the potentially offending parent! While taking out stress and aggression on a child by punching them or locking them in a closet or not feeding them or committing other heinous acts against them should be punishable, arresting parents for 'threats' and slaps on the derriere is a frightening retribution thereby limiting the effectiveness of being a parent (once again, that ethereal 'middle ground' of strict-but-fair is quite difficult). Not bluffing when it comes to following up on punishment, not giving in when the child begs or whines, not worrying whether or not you're as popular in your child's mind as his/her celebrity idols, feeding your child/children three square meals and making sure they don't live in filth, checking to make sure they do their homework correctly, that they wake up on time to go to school: these are the requirements for being a parent. Or maybe some teachers are right: maybe there should be such a thing as "parent school" where adults learn how to praise and punish and love. Oh, those utopian ideals!

11. Pregnancy, Dress Codes and the 'Last Taboo.'

—Survey of High School graduates: 17.7% of males and 82.2% of females reported sexual harassment by faculty or staff during their school careers. 13.5% of those surveyed said they had engaged in sexual intercourse with a teacher. (Wishnietsky, "Reported and Unreported Teacher-Student Sexual Harassment", Journal of Ed Research, Vol. 3, 1991, pp. 164-69)

It was certainly one of the most surreal moments of my teaching life: 8th grade, class of thirteen kids, two pregnant and one out on 'maternity.' I just sat there awestruck: they're children, and they're having children. This may have been the norm in times past, but they're so immature and essentially helpless in this 'modern age' that the idea of them reproducing before they've even gotten to High School can't help but make one just a tad uncomfortable. At 14 - which was how old the girls were - I wasn't even very good at tying my own tie that was required for my High School uniform.

With the increasing sexualization of the young it shouldn't be surprising that yes, girls are getting pregnant and yes, teens are having sex. In one reality-shaking moment, the students of one class in E— Middle School were flinging condom packets at each other in class - I had to intervene and tell them to put them away (one girl assured me, "We're going to use them later" - whether she was kidding or not isn't the issue, at least she's being safe).

If the students are having sex with each other, why should it be so surprising that in multiple well known incidents, it was teachers 'crossing the line' - Mary Kay Letourneau (who had sex with a 13-year-old Samoan-American boy who she later married), Pamela Turner (a physical education teacher who had sex with a 13-year-old boy), Debra Lafave (who had sex with a 14-year-old boy) the list goes on - that have drawn so much attention. The 'taboo' of these incidents, combined with the fact that the teachers were *female* added to their news appeal and the need for society to pretend to shock itself.

Recent stories of pedophilia (focusing on pre-teens) and ephebophilia (focusing on teenagers) - the two are frequently confused - have been discussed with absolute hysteria, and society operates on these double standards: teenage girls are scantily dressed and used to sell clothing, music and so on, but actually desiring them is shameful (the marketing taps into repressed desires). There's a sense of touching on the forbidden in breaking what could be called 'the last taboo' - that of illicit child love - and 'breaking' that law can be likened to a thrill crime, an exercise in adrenaline. Parents who genuinely worry about their children should be aware that actual perverts and crazies do exist, and that - once again - being a parent involves being active in your child's life, like nosing around in their 'business' and checking up on them. Parents who pride themselves on being parents should also be aware of what their children are wearing, and not permit their young teenage daughters to wear short shorts, for example, that have elaborate writings, lipstick marks or any attention getting slogans ("Cheer!") on their rears to draw the attention of others. I have no problem with teenagers getting used to themselves as sexual beings - which we all are - but this is a form of 'advertisement' in which the (presumably male) gaze is drawn towards the posterior.

I have noticed, without offering much commentary to others about it for fear of being looked upon suspiciously, a real lack of reinforcement of dress codes in the middle and high schools - the trend during my tenure was for girls to wear what could only be described as nightwear (pajamas, to be exact) during school time. Some of them even carry with them stuffed animals and blankets for when they get "cold." As a male in a sensitive position, I was hesitant to say anything about the one girl I noticed at B— Middle School whose pajama top didn't have a lot of buttons and one of her breasts was actually exposed. Instead of saying something (to which someone else could respond, "How did you notice?"), I pretended I didn't see a thing and avoided going near her. The other students never said anything. Saying nothing is wise.

Some of the 'summer' attire - again, for the girls only - was revealing. I had to pass out notices from Vice-Principals and such in homerooms in Middle School explaining exactly what could and could not be worn, but the girls blithely ignored the mandates, coming in with tight-fitting tops, bared midriffs and short shorts. It's as if the Dress Code paper was a guideline to be used on *what* to wear in the morning ("Wait, that dress is too long … it says we can't expose more than 6" above our knee so that means we have to go shorter"). One girl who was very popular with the boys - they told me "she throws the best parties" and I just shrugged - wore a tight red top that said "I've got issues," as if having issues was a point of pride and acceptance in this at times very skewed world. Male teachers, like myself, seem to stay away from addressing the problems for fear of sexual harassment labels and embarrassment and headaches.

High schools are the places you'd expect overt sexual behavior, and it's the custodians who have told me that they've caught students behind the bleachers in the gym after school hours making out and whatnot. Instead of being embarrassed when caught - which would logically be the natural human reaction to be caught in an intimate moment - it's one of rage, with the students caught denying what it is they were doing, then lashing out at the custodians, claiming they were intentionally spying on them, when the custodians were merely doing their jobs. As expected, no punishment was given to the mischievous students who were clearly trespassing on school grounds after hours.

One former substitute who actually got a full-time teaching gig in one of the elementary schools told me during lunch that one day she was substituting at L— High School, for something like 11th grade math. One of the boys in the class was getting very friendly, asking her if she wanted to go out after school for something to eat, and making a scene in front of the whole class. This substitute told the student that if he didn't stop bothering her and interfering with her teaching, she was going to write him up. The kid called her bluff, and sticking to her word, she wrote him up. Hilariously, the student was appalled by this, went straight to the Principal, who, after hearing the student's 'side,' *revoked* the detention (or whatever it is she wrote him up for), telling this young lady that "boys will be boys" and writing them up for "playful advancement" didn't solve anything. She was so irate she refused to ever set foot in that place again, with a Principal who wants to be a Friend and not a Disciplinarian who backs his staff.

So with students being so *sexualized*, the idea of teacher-student relations isn't so completely unrealistic, although certainly a problem that, if arises, has to be dealt with calm and cool behavior. I've even heard of a substitute teacher who was asked not to return to a certain Middle School because of making 'lewd gestures' towards the girls and was so disgusted by the charge he sought legal action against the District. I never saw him around again, so I don't know what happened to him. Most of the teachers I knew were upstanding individuals in this department, aware of the boundaries between their students and them. I also observed a certain boundary line between teachers and each other, dispelling the mistaken fantasies of student life that so-and-so teachers were dating each other behind their spouses' backs and that this teacher actually had a crush on that one. Admit it: you conjured fictional narratives about your own teachers as well. Fantasies are generally healthy and normal, but precisely that: products of the active mind. There's a degree of self-control required on both sides: for teachers who presume that they can 'get away with it' and that a relationship with a minor is rewarding in any other way but physical pleasure, and for the students to curtail their sometimes overly forward behavior, which could possibly lead some teachers astray. I dismiss the claim that all these adolescents are mere bystanders caught up in the passions of an adult, and that a good percentage of them are flattered by the attention of an older, more mature figure.

Besides from being sexualized, however - and certainly brazen about it - it seems as if they're taking steps earlier and earlier into a life of criminal activity. Although not 'taboo' in the strictest sense, this story rattled the teachers of the Middle School who I told it to: I was at a local mall with two friends, playing games in the arcade and killing time before we had to leave to meet up with other friends who were getting out of work. We were both waiting for one particular game to be freed up, when a girl walked in that I instantly recognized: she was an 8th grade student from E— Middle School, and with her was a well-dressed, well-groomed young man with a Yankees hat on and a black jacket. She came up to me with surprise and exclaimed, "It's Mr. Lovie!" (it was a 'joke name' the students in her class came up with for me). We started 'talking' - and I mean this in the loosest sense - as I was asking her questions and she was staring into my eyes.

"Are you high?" she kept asking me, and I kept insisting I wasn't, but she kept looking closely anyway, even noticing my contact lenses. I asked what she was doing in the mall, and she ignored my questions, telling me about her boyfriend, who was already in High School. Then, and this is disturbing, she asked if we wanted drugs, because both her and her boyfriend were selling. I told them no, we're set, and they ran out of the arcade and sat on a bench outside. When we left the arcade, they were still sitting there, and I waved bye to them, promising I wouldn't tell anyone what they were doing.

I lied a little, telling a few of the teachers from her school that could be trusted and that would believe me. Most were shocked and immediately asked for a name, but I did keep my word and not say anything. *She* was the one that looked like she was on drugs, being pulled around by her charismatic boyfriend, and it was at once humorous and chillingly tragic - that of a 15-year-old already dabbling in criminal activity. One of the people I spoke to about it followed up my story with the question, "I wonder if she was for sale?" Though it sounds crass, in times like these with teenagers like these, it wasn't completely out-of-line. "Frankly," I responded, "I don't even want to know."

12. Everybody Left Behind.

The 2002 No Child Left Behind Act, one of the many beguiling products of the George W. Bush administration and the gemstone that was intended to 'fix' our educational system, has been met with understandable hostility from teachers and critics. There are essentially two goals of the action that warrant attention: (1.) to improve the teachers who teach the "core" subjects (English, reading or language arts, math, science, the foreign languages, civics/government, economics and the arts) so they can be labeled "highly qualified." Those 'exempt' are the physical education teachers, counselors, librarians and nurses. This also means that a teacher must be fully certified, i.e. not have an "emergency certificate" like I have. Goal (2.) is that by the idealistic year of 2014, all minorities and students from low-income families can read and do math at their proper grade level, hence the very title of the law (which has since been "replaced" by the Every Student Succeeds Act).

The idealism of the project - just as the Bush administration's wartime idealism, in freeing the Middle East from corruption and winning hearts and minds of a people who resent American imperialism - is admittedly nice in a very naïve way. Yes, it would be splendid if all teachers were extra qualified to put that extra effort in to educating 'difficult' students with bad home lives or a poor understanding of English, and yes, it would be nice if the gap between the gifted and not-gifted was made smaller through extra devotion and time. But idealism doesn't produce results, and neither do budgetary constraints, with school districts and the N.E.A. (National Education Association) complaining that the government is not shelling out enough money to pay for the elaborate nature of the project. The Bush administration had already spent billions on the initiative, but the billions spent have been absorbed by the price of yearly testing and making sure teachers are "highly qualified."

Based on personal experience, I can say that it sounds like the initiative is placing entirely too much blame for America's poor standing academically in the civilized world on the teachers themselves, inferring that a good portion of them are not "highly qualified" and that the very process of teaching is a figurative arrow pointing in one direction: from teacher to student(s). It's sensible to say that teachers need to be "highly qualified" in their respective fields, but the logic of the No Child Left Behind statement is: there are children who are struggling in school from low-income families and in minority brackets, so therefore their *teachers* need to be "better educated" to meet these demands. It says nothing about the students themselves, of their attitude towards studying, of their home lives, of the incentives created for them to have the desire to excel in school. It's as if the government figures are saying we can't fix the American Family, so let's fix the American Educator.

Based on my time teaching grades K-12, I have noticed one rampant, raging problem among all students, no matter what race: *laziness*. I had a student in a 4th grade class at W— Elementary School who wouldn't get his books out, wouldn't write anything down with a pencil, wouldn't budge, just stared at the wall in front of him. The school psychologist stopped by and I pointed out this boy to him, who I was under the impression was ill in some way, or autistic. The psychologist rolled his eyes and whispered to me, "He's not autistic. We tested him. He's f-u-c-k-i-n-g l-a-z-y."

I've been in classes where over half the class didn't have pencils, didn't have notebooks, didn't have rulers. Students just sat down and did nothing. Some teachers realized this, wised up, and started giving out rulers with cartoon characters on them, odd-looking pencils with dragons, glitter pens … *anything* to have them take even a modicum of interest in the supplies required to do work. Despite all that, the kids would *still* say they left their pencils or rulers or papers at home (this is not to be confused with the sad fact that at many schools they didn't have enough actual books for the students to read, so they had to share, but the district was spending millions on laptops, after all: smart investment). One Middle School teacher had the right idea: the student that didn't have his/her pencils, books or paper had to stand the entire class in the corner of the room as punishment. I'm surprised he never got called on this, what with our fear of having our precious youngsters "humiliated" in front of their peers.

Often times teachers would leave me stacks of worksheets that I had to give out to the classes, and the kids would refuse to do them. I would tell them - reading off the substitute plans - that the work was going to be collected and graded at the end of class, but that didn't faze a good percentage of the students. "I'm failing already," some of them would say. At the end of the class I collected the papers like I said I would, and even on an 8th grade level the answers would be sentence fragments or hastily scribbled guesses. Not having to grade the papers myself, I couldn't say how the regular teacher responded to such scribble-scratch. I guess as long as they turned something in, that would ensure that they could be passed, and that was all that mattered.

It's important to state the following: this laziness I've noticed is not defined to a particular race or even gender. It was a daily constant I kept encountering, school to school, like a social epidemic. Even kids in 'advanced classes' were 'bored' with the work and would give the least amount of effort on it or not do it at all. At F— High School, I was teaching an English class, and I gave an assignment to do over the weekend. The one student told me he wasn't going to do it, and would negotiate with the teacher on Monday as to why he didn't do it. "It worked before," he told me, suggesting that this teacher could be "bargained" with. Likewise, not all of the students who are academically challenged just sit there, waiting impatiently for their "F's." Some of them do work extremely hard. In one startling example, at B— Elementary, there was a young student that needed Learning Support for reading: he was from Beijing, and was doing poorly in English. I sat with this boy for an entire class period, and he would get so worked up over not understanding, say, subjects and predicates, he would start *perspiring* ... sweating all over his notebook. His mother and the Learning Support teacher had a written communication going on in his daily planner in which the L.S. teacher wrote about his progress during the day, and the mother would write at night what work he did at home. Granted, not all parents are this involved, but they should be.

I tried asking some of the students if they cared, when they wouldn't do their worksheets that were going to be graded or just threw together whatever sloppy answers down on a quiz I was told to give them. Honestly, a lot of them appeared - to me, at least - to be entirely apathetic, most shrugging it off like it was just a secondary thing. I was told by some that they'd "pass anyway," because that's what always happened. This bothered me deeply, because it showed that they knew that they were being pushed through, that the teachers *had* to push them through. The teachers tried to keep their part of the deal, but the students just slid on by.

It's certainly no mystery that a portion of middle and high school students are involved to some degree with drugs and/or alcohol. The most telling declaration of their condition was by, of all people, a Middle School Principal during his final year. He was in a meeting with a gentleman I knew who worked as the school's in-house computer support technician. Some students drifted by when they were talking, and the Principal looked over to them, laughed and said, "All these kids want to do is go home and smoke pot." The man who was with him was understandably floored by this utterance, since it's the last thing he expected the *Principal* to say, and wasn't sure if it was conjecture or whimsy or what the statement really meant - was he speaking figuratively? Was he convinced it was actually true?

I was able, during the summers, to gain extra money when not teaching working with some students from one of the high schools to clean and update the software on the computers in the different buildings. After an icy reception, they warmed up to me and I to them, and we got to talking about high school life and, inevitably, the drug use of their peers. The fact that a potentially alarming number of High School students either drink, do drugs or both is not surprising to me: in fact, a good number of my peers in high school did a lot of drugs and drank a lot of alcohol. But is it really so plausible that drugs/alcohol are a catch-all for high school woes? Or are they merely a small factor in a much larger stew of personal and social problems?

Having spent so much time with 8th graders - not by my own volition, but because the Sub Caller, Batty, would only send me to those grades because no one else wanted them (and not call me for weeks if I turned any particular job down) - I can only say that, by age 14 or 15 (15 if the student repeated a grade along the way), the students already realized whether or not they could excel in the system or not, whether or not they were "good at" school. Those that could succeed usually kept up, while the rest seemed resigned to their mediocrity. 8th grade is a tough grade to teach. Not being completely ignorant of life, they realized at this point that school offered nothing to them, that doing any work, no matter how simple, was just meaningless. Why bother even *thinking* about something that could do you little good? If you keep doing poorly at something - for me, it's definitely Physics - interest in it wanes; few can stay interested in something if they don't "get it" to some degree.

Perhaps an option would be to create an alternate schooling system, one that recognizes this discrepancy. Although 14 or 15 is a little too young to decide on life goals, it's clear at that point if the students are college bound or not. I was covering a Learning Support class at E— Middle School, and made a point to break that distance I usually employed with the students to ask the class, who threw the papers they had to work on in the recycling bin, exactly why they didn't care. One of the boys in the class who I knew from way back in Elementary School told me that when he "got out" of school he was going to work with his brother at his garage. He figured this is what he was destined to do, maybe he'd find something like it in VoTech (vocational and technical training) - a good program that needs to be expanded for students who are not designed for the basic school curriculum - and go with that.

I'm positive that it isn't entirely the teachers' fault if the students do poorly or struggle with English: there's only so much time in the day and will-power in the student. You can have the teachers continue to take extra classes after school - 'freshen up' courses - and you can set up special initiatives so that the students can work with laptops, so that students who are struggling can be placed in smaller classes so they get extra one-on-one time with the teacher. You can increase, increase, increase spending. You can make sure the teachers are very good at what they do and devoted to their jobs. But you can't change the backgrounds of the kids who are having difficulties, forcing them to work, getting them the attention after school to make sure they do their homework and that the homework is checked correctly, you can't help it if the parents don't speak English and therefore the students with a poor understanding of English will never become proficient with the language. The *No Child Left Behind Act*, now "defunct," made a little bit of sense in theory. But theories can't pay for after-school tutors, strong parental supervision and guidance, language fluency and the all-important incentives to learn.

13. The Easy Work (When You Can Get It).

It would be extremely brutal and one-sided to infer that every day I substituted over the course of several years was agony. In fact, timing, luck and caution sometimes gave me a string of very good days that were easy and relatively painless. It usually depended on what kind of teacher I went in for and what school I was at. For example, taking a 5th grade class at some schools with a good deal of not quite academically inclined students or those from low-income neighborhoods was probably not going to be easy, plain and simple. Taking a 4th grade class at a school with mostly middle-class kids and a strict but fair teacher who strongly punished those that misbehaved for a substitute was probably going to be pain-free.

I found that certain subjects allowed for easier days as a substitute, and jumped at them at a moment's notice. Covering for art class, physical education, the 'gifted' classes or learning support *in some schools* was often simple and straightforward. Don't get me wrong: Once I was in for physical education at a particular Elementary School and had to break up a near-riot - or the closest you could get to a riot among eleven-year-olds - in which the class was beating up on two of their classmates for playing a prank on them earlier in the day. I had to step in, try to protect the kids being kicked in the face and take them to the office. I had such a headache after that incident that I conducted class from the rest of the day seated in a chair nursing a coffee, waiting for the Tylenol the nurse gave me to start working and blowing a whistle instead of yelling when I wanted their attention.

For the most part, kids in Elementary School *adore* gym class. Adore. They love to run around, scream and 'fake fall' onto the ground or into each other. They also love kickball. Give a class of twenty-five a kickball, lean against the wall and let them run around the bases. Before I knew it, their regular teacher was standing at the entrance to the gym, waiting for his/her class. The fantastic thing about being in for gym, too, was being able to tell the teacher directly that a particular student was misbehaving. When students would get rough or violent if they were losing in some nonsense game and yell at their peers, I would sit them down in the corner, forbidding them to participate until they calmed down (when their teachers came in, I'd tell them directly about the misbehavior, and let them deal with it). Sometimes, the students I'd sit out for gym for behavior problems would be so upset about missing gym - the gym they crave - they'd start *crying* and pleading with me to let them back in. They start hating gym in Middle School and High School, where they don't have time to shower and therefore smell the rest of the day, but in Elementary School, smelling bad is part of the fun.

I've also found that teaching Learning Support in some of the Elementary Schools has been a breeze. One day, I swear, I worked with two students for half the day and had the other half of the day free to read the book I always brought with me. I understand from the Learning Support teachers that doing it full time - with the baggage of dealing with the parents of these slow learners, not to mention the slow learners themselves - was a nuisance, and one in particular - a former classmate of mine - left Learning Support to go back to teach a 'regular' class. But from the level of a substitute, Learning Support was perfect. I loved it. All day I worked with a handful of kids at a small desk - it was the closest to one-on-one work you could get. I could always deal with a group of five kids reading a story versus a class of 27. With most Learning Support classes, I had tiny groups and simple lesson plans: lots of worksheets. If they were bad during Learning Support class, I'd just send them back to their homerooms and their regular teachers (although this was rare). There was a school or two (C— Elementary, D— Elementary) that had much larger LS rooms - between 20 or 25 each - and those could be tricky: two dozen academically stunted individuals at the same time. That was no fun, so I figured out which schools had 'smaller' L.S. classes and stuck with those.

Another perk of Learning Support was co-teaching. Most Learning Support instructors spent a part of their day in the same room as another teacher, thereby dividing the class into two parts and making the burden lighter on both. Sometimes the regular teacher whom I had to co-teach with wouldn't have anything for me to do, so he/she'd just sit me at a table in the back of the room with a student who was having difficulty with some assignment. If the student didn't 'get it' after working with me, it was no big deal. If the Learning Support students didn't finish their assignments, it was never a big deal. It was expected.

In our District, it was imperative that one didn't confuse Learning Support with Emotional Support: they're two different scenarios. Emotional Support consisted of smallish classes, but unlike the kids in L.S., were mentally ill. Now, no one ever wanted to use the words "mentally ill," but it's true. If a child is placed in the E.S. classes, he/she is disturbed. Period. One Principal at an Elementary School that won't be named told me he'll never forget the day when *I* was covering a physical education class at his school, and one of the E.S. kids that was in my class ran from the gym to his office, grabbing a pair of scissors on the way and threatening to do physical harm to everyone, including him. This Principal had to lock the boy in his office before the police could show up - although it was scary, it was also ridiculous and absurd to leave school that day with police squad cars sitting outside the school with the officers themselves inside the building, given the task of calming the boy down and removing him from the building (they also brought in an ambulance, which scared the other children). Other E.S. classes had students who would physically pummel each other, not understand limits/boundaries and sometimes undress in class (one girl grabbed my leg and would not let go - I had to actually ... and I hate admitting this ... 'pry' her off my leg using a folder). They saw no problem with shouting expletives at their teachers and threatened the other kids in the school. Oh, and a few threw chairs at the walls for fun.

I've tried avoiding the Special Ed. classes in the high schools because of horror stories from others, and figured it was bad enough dealing with actual high school students and all their problems, much less Special Ed. One substitute that tried it told me that they had Teacher Assistants in the rooms who, if the kids were good, would allow them to watch *Jerry Springer* as a reward. Though you'd think this is horrible as a 'treat,' they actually loved it and sat in awe of the individuals on the screen. This fellow sub told me, "It was like they were watching themselves." She told me she'd jump and do it at a moment's notice, but she was in the minority: most others warned me against it. I was only in for Special Ed. one time at F— High School and for about an hour (I had to cover for another teacher) - in that time the Teacher Assistant told them they could either watch *The SpongeBob SquarePants Movie* or sleep. Those that watched the movie loved it and laughed right along (as did I) and those that didn't rested on the floor.

Some have advised me to throw a movie into the classroom TV in case the classroom teacher gave me some bullshit instructions like "Have class read silently for 45 minutes." 45 minutes? Silently read? With a substitute? Were they out of their heads? At least if I put a movie in, they'd settle down. But more often than not, I couldn't find a classroom TV or a movie in the classroom they could watch. To make it easier on myself, I'd manufacture work from the class text book and tell them I'm collecting it for a quiz grade. There was no way reading for 45 minutes with raging teenagers was going to work, so if I lied and made up work for them, I figured at least half the class would bother themselves with working on it, meaning the room would be half as loud as if none of them had any work. It was all about cutting losses.

With regards to general behavior as a substitute, there are some things I do advise. They are as follows:

1. Even if you don't complete everything in the sub plan, write down that you tried. Teachers have come down on me hard for not completing little things on their sub plans, as if the ten minutes between me arriving and school starting was sufficient for me to decipher the way they run their classes, find their books and sort everything out. Sometimes you get sub plans that are elaborate and sometimes you get sub plans that are threadbare and often incorrect. Be prepared to distract the kids if you're stuck on something.

2. I don't care what anyone tells you and I can't reiterate this enough: be very cautious about eating in the faculty room. I only did if I had to, like the classroom was being taken up by some other teachers. If you have to eat in the faculty room, be quiet. Don't complain or ask questions - act like everything's going well. I've asked questions and all but been told, "It's not your problem" or when I've asked "what's wrong with" a student, I would get ignored. These teachers are very often embittered and hostile, especially mid-day. Be careful who you try to befriend. Not all of them will like you, but that's the way it goes. I know teachers are not supposed to eat in the classrooms, but I always did, and no one complained to me. In the faculty room, they have seats they sit in every day, so ask politely

if you're sitting in someone's seat - I've already been asked to move. Once you're hired full-time, naturally, you'll be expected to be in there.

3. Coffee in the faculty room isn't free, but I make sure it's free for me. They have these "coffee clubs" and make you pay anywhere from a quarter to a dollar for a cup if you aren't in the club. I've already poured myself coffee, not paid the money, and been told before walking out of the faculty room that the coffee "wasn't free" by another teacher in the room who was eyeing me. I then would put my money in the cup ... and take it out later in the day when no one was in the faculty room and put it back in my pocket. You know what that meant? *Fuck you*, that's what that meant. I put up with all this nonsense and then I have to pay $.50 for a cheap, burnt cup of Folgers?

4. Playing meek and apologetic is good. It's true. Apologize to teachers, secretaries, Principals all day. Teachers like it when you kowtow to them and play to their egos, which get trampled on every day by little pipsqueaks and know-it-alls. They don't want to hear defensiveness or difficulty in your substitute voice. They want you to apologize and squirm and make excuses. If they want to lash at you, you have to take it. Apologize some more.

5. Don't call the office too often for problems, because after a while they'll get sick of you and either tell you to deal with it, to learn how to "discipline a class" or something to that effect. Or they'll tell the sub callers never to send you back, which is fine if you could care less about being a full-time teacher. Learn your own ways for getting through the day, which basically means swallowing bullshit and allowing yourself to be humiliated by children. Remember, in the 'chain,' as a substitute, you're an outsider, and beneath everyone.

6. Learn the good schools from the bad schools. Keep lists of what classes were good. This ensures good days. Find which schools work best for you. If you have a string

of bad days at a school, it's not worth it to torture yourself by going back there over and over again. This is common sense. Ask the other substitutes, if you talk to them, about their experiences. You will also encounter some regular teachers who are open-minded and highly sympathetic: milk them for information, and they will most likely help you out or tell you what they've heard (that's how I received a good deal of my information, not to mention details about things going on in the schools that they try to "hush up"). I was already in for a 5th grade teacher at R— Elementary that was so efficient, the sub plans read, "The class will conduct itself," and to my shock, it did. The teacher managed to subdivide duties among the kids in lieu of her absence and the details and instructions were on the board for them. I was able to sit in front of the room and take it easy while they did the problems in their books and handed out their own worksheets and checked each others' quizzes. It was … amazing. It was the educational ideal.

14. Woe to the Naïve, or The Case of the Missing Red Ink.

I feel bad for teachers who are coming out of college all doe-eyed like characters in Japanese cartoons, ready and willing to teach future generations, to make a major difference in the lives of hundreds - if not thousands - of students. That's certainly the propaganda these Departments of Education push onto the young and impressionable. I cannot tell you how many times I've subbed for a teacher, and in that same class there was a Student Teacher from one of the local colleges, putting in his/her time as an apprentice for graduation, bounding with joy at being around kids and being able to teach. Talking to me was like talking to the voice they didn't want to hear: I would recant stories like the ones I've documented here, and the Student Teacher would either not believe me, or immediately blame me and question my place in the stories ("You just weren't *firm* enough with them"), like I somehow encouraged the ill-behavior. I've spoken with young women outside of school that work in grocery stores or at retail stores who are early on in their collegiate careers and free to tell me they "love children" and about all the times they babysat or worked part-time with one or two kids at the hospital. "One or two kids is not a classroom of 25," I would say, but my words of warning weren't enough to crack their devotion. When one young woman I warned about teaching finally finished up her Student Teaching, and had a 3rd grade class that was crawling around on the floor and belligerent ("Why are they crawling on the floors?" she asked me. "Can't they walk?"), *then* it dawned on her. Some of it hits much later: the second or third year of teaching has gone, and that's when they realize they have twenty eight more to go, and that *shiver* of panic hits them.

I place a portion of the blame on the Educational Departments in colleges for not giving their own students a serious, strict heads up on all this (and not actively combating their potential delusions of teaching grandeur), and I never even went through a program of any sort, so I walked in with absolutely no expectations or ideals. A little dose of sober reality needs to be a part of that program, and not a single student teacher I met was prepared for potential crises. Others that have been doing it a while seem to agree. My Mom would tell me about when she was at college preparing to earn her teaching certificate, and they'd do these classroom exercises *with their peers*, and how deceptively easy it was to 'instruct' a group of 20-year-old college students to collaborate on building a paper castle versus 'instructing' a group of 20 ten-year-olds - who maybe don't want to build a paper castle and aren't paying money to be in school - to do the same thing. My Mom didn't feel like she was adequately prepared for the harsh reality of the day-to-day monotony of the job, of the pressure from the other teachers, of late-night phone calls from the parents. Back in the 1970's it was stressful on her - she couldn't imagine it today.

Callow teachers aren't properly warned about the politics of the system, of how little support you might receive from other teachers or the administration, of the rampant behavior problems. Some of the young teachers I worked with at B— Middle School were trying to get pregnant just so they didn't have to teach. There's a loophole in the system that can be - and has been - exploited: one teacher in particular taught for six months and then got pregnant; then she took a year's maternity leave and when it was time to return, she became pregnant again. This happened *four times*, and became a joke among the employees of the Human Resources office and the District itself.

If a portion of the blame gets placed on the government and another portion on the Educational Department in the Universities producing the teachers that statistically leave in large numbers by their fifth year teaching, another percentage of the blame needs to be placed on the institution itself, the individuals within the institutions and the Districts themselves. Some educators have apparently become so exhausted trying to mollycoddle these wild, shameless, lazy students, they can't think straight. One frequently posted article became a joke amongst myself and my friends: in April 2005, and I'm not sure who conceived of this, some ding-a-ling decided that using red ink to grade tests and essays was too "stressful" on the students, the very color being too harsh on their eyeballs and brains. The Principal of Thaddeus Stevens Elementary School in Pittsburgh, Joseph Foriska, was quoted as saying that, "You could hold up a paper that says 'Great work!' and it won't matter if it's written in red" and encouraged teachers to use what he called pens or markers with "pleasant-feeling tones" to grade papers and leave comments.

You know what? There's more! In April 2005, in USA Today, a report by Larry Copeland said that students were being paid for "tattling on their peers," for telling on other students about guns or drugs. This has bled into our own District - there's currently a "hotline" for tips, which will no doubt be abused. This same April of 2005, thirteen laptops were stolen from E— Middle School by students after school: the total bill for the laptops was close to $20,000. In response, the Principal of the school and Administration, in their brilliance, decided to offer a $500 reward for information that led to the recovery of the laptops. Now, the Administration and Superintendent were not in the school the day the mention of Reward Money was announced, but *I* was, and the students were hysterical. In between delivering the message to the students over the PA system and walking up the steps to the second floor of the building, the Principal was stopped by four (yes, four) students ready to give up names. That wasn't all: students were planning meetings with him and the guidance counselors and the Vice Principals, all-too-eager to rat each other out. This was creating tension in the hallways and classrooms, where the students didn't like being accused by their peers, and some kids that had nothing to do with it were getting hostile with those accusing them. The paranoia was a disruption, and the school was turned into something like Arthur Miller's *The Crucible*. When one of the students that was late to class gave me a pass from the Principal, he said he was sure he was going to get the reward so he could get the new game system by Sony.

What came of the interrogations? Nothing. The laptops were never recovered. I was informed, by someone that works at the school, that the District's lawyers warned them against further questioning and 'accusations,' because of fear of the "students' rights." I'm sorry, but stealing thirteen computers is a crime, and by not working overtime to find the perpetrators, you're merely encouraging more theft. If no one's going to be punished, why not commit the crime? The police said that unless the students are caught with the devices in hand, there was nothing much you could do. I wonder how pleased the city's taxpayers would be if they thought about how their money's going to pay for the replacements?

I was bothered by the decision to leave the detective work to the students themselves, but not everyone was in agreement with me. One teacher in particular told me she thought it was a good thing, and that way the kids were 'policing themselves.' This sounded to me like an admission that the teachers and administration were out of touch with their schools, so why not let the kids create a

113

system of checks on each other? "Snitching," in the mob, leads to horrific consequences, so why it should work among teenagers makes little sense to me, but if it is a successful tactic and there are no internal problems, well then don't mind me, Goody Proctor.

It does comfort me, in some very basic way, to know that the United States isn't alone in having problems with students. The U.K.'s been experiencing the same thing. An article that was printed in *The Times* back in April (that month again) 2003 said that the Government was planning to invest £470 million over the following three years in a "new national behavior and attendance strategy." The writer of the piece, Sally Morris, cites a statistic that said that of 2,500 teachers questioned, 80% "thought that standards of behavior have deteriorated during their time in teaching and that even children in nursery schools are now displaying high levels of unacceptable actions."

A suggestion made by the article came from an educational psychologist by the name of Joan Freeman from Middlesex University, who said that "teachers need to be trained in the psychology of control - this does not mean excluding children from school activities, but introducing incentives and rewards for acceptable behavior ... I think that we all expect too much of teachers." Professor Freeman is right, in theory - the need to use psychology to 'combat' the children is a good suggestion, but it didn't always help me. Why? Classroom size, for one: it's easier to settle down a handful of kids rather than a class of twenty-five or so, where your attention is going in all sorts of directions, from students who appear right along side you asking the most ridiculous of questions to those that are asking to use the bathroom to those that are confused by the assignment you've just given them.

Although it's unreasonable on any logical level, the ideal ratio would be about seven students for every one teacher, with multiple teachers in the room working with their 'set' of children. Some classrooms have ballooned in size from twenty-five to thirty, and they're crammed into the rooms. As I wrote before, the easiest days - for me, at least - were the ones where I had smaller numbers of students (Learning Support) or was allowed to let them run and scream free (Physical Education in Elementary Schools) or had them working on some painting project that 'turned off' their thinking and allowed them just to have fun and be focused (Art class) that proved to be the most manageable.

With the turnover rate as it is, it's plenty clear that teachers are generally a discontent lot (I've seen so many 'new' teachers bolt in a few years' time). Without completely disillusioning future generations of teachers, what's left to say to them, faced with a career that might not be what they expect? Are they aware that the 'system' they work under isn't helping them, but hurting them? Do they have the determination to stick with it and stay the course? Or does Marketing sound like a more reasonable option, what with the continuous rise of big business? At least when you work for a *Fortune 500* company, you'll probably never have to worry about being spit on by a nine-year-old, called at night by an irate parent or called in for meetings with the Principal about your poor "class management" skills. You'll only have to worry about being laid off.

15. I'm Not Going To Take This Any More?

"There was a time when parents who came
into school to see staff about a problem
asked what their child had done. Now they
ask what the school has done to their child."

- An anonymous teacher, Leeds, UK

All those years were enough for me to get in, take a look around, wonder what in the hell I was doing with my time, and then get out. I've always been astounded, in recanting these stories and anecdotes to other non-teachers, how they look at me dumbfounded and incredulous. They have no idea. I've often used the word "degraded" in talking about it to friends, acquaintances and strangers, which was how I felt. The system, complex and formidable, wears you down. Sure, I was a substitute, and they treat substitutes worse than their regular teachers, but they still treat everyone bad - for me, it was *amplified*. After one day I would be exhausted, but I'm confident that the result of a regular teacher's five-day week, with all its nuisance problems, failing test scores and meetings, has the same cumulative effect. One bonus of being in my shoes was that I got a taste of it all - I subbed in every single building in our entire District - without the commitment: towards the end, I learned not to involve myself to *any* degree in the job, to be a shell of a person standing in front of the disinterested hordes, just muttering the details listed in the lesson plans and letting them do their work. Powerless to keep them from hassling me, I was also powerless to stop them from hassling each other, bearing witness to cruel behavior by students against students.

Nothing other than actually doing the job itself can prepare you for the complexity of it. The Hollywood movies that show low-income or inner-city problem kids 'aided' by the system (*To Sir, With Love, Dangerous Minds, Lean on Me, Blackboard Jungle* and so many more) are fine and quaint and idyllic - teachers 'correcting' the wayward, growing in mutual respect, etc. - but not always the closest approximation to reality. The 'truth' of the situation isn't always pleasant or pretty with the prerequisite Hollywood ending. There's a cycle at play:

Single parent has no time for child(ren), too busy trying to work to support everyone. Parents from stressful jobs, plagued with drinking/drug problems, unhappy and depressed, neglect to pass love onto their own children who come to school unloved and themselves unhappy with their home lives. Kids lead other kids down problem paths, or kids looking for acceptance join gangs. Kids from privileged families know they can do no wrong, have inflated egos, realize that their parents will back them no matter what.

Kids come to school and have no respect, no fear, no sense of embarrassment at being fools, of no desire to 'succeed' in the world. Teachers, themselves under pressure from Principals, annoying parents, government oversight and so on have to work overtime to make up for lost time due to constant disciplining, endless 'team meetings,' and lesson planning. If there's a serious discipline problem, their hands - and the hands of the administration - are proverbially 'tied' by children's rights and potential legal trouble, so therefore some teachers are hesitant to properly reprimand students for fear of incurring more problems on themselves. Lawyers run America, and nobody wants to deal with that.

If students think a teacher said something wrong, or 'bad,' or 'humiliated' them, or didn't grade their test correctly, they tell their parents who call the school, immediately assessing blame instead of taking the school's side. The Principals, scared of the parents and the administration, come down on the only people they can come down on: the teachers. The stress, like in the dysfunctional family unit, has to be dispersed somehow - the parents take it out on their children; the Principals on their teachers. The teachers, in return, become nitpicky and difficult towards each other (particularly as the year goes on), substitutes and the students. How do you fix the system without individually repairing the pieces? Is it too tangled a mess to solve? Is the institution of education, like Joseph Heller's depiction of war, another Catch-22?

Ultimately, the wrong people are Afraid. Fear is misdirected. The teachers are afraid of the students, parents and Principals, the Principals are afraid of the parents and administration and the administration is afraid of the parents' lawyers. Who's not afraid? The students. Left unchecked, they are actually running this whole charade into the ground. They have entirely too many rights, they are unafraid of being punished because the punishments are weak and ineffectual and often not enforced, and their very parents have set their children on the highest peak, standing behind them, wanting so desperately to be young again and 'popular' in the eyes of their children instead of proper disciplinarians. Somewhere, someone has to start issuing some kind of proper punishment and not back down.

Although I'm not someone who can see into the future and predict where all this is going to go, something has to be done. If it can't be done in the American family, it has to be done in the schools. There are police officers in some of the buildings, but they're mostly decoration, like cardboard cutouts. The kids don't see the incentives of learning, and if the portrait of the future we paint for them isn't appealing and of no value, then they should experience first hand what hard labor is. They should have to clean bathrooms. They should see what it's like to work like a slave in a sweatshop where other children in the world toil on a daily basis, having *their* childhoods robbed from them (by acting the way they do, squandering what they're given, they're indirectly slapping all these other children in the face). Preaching rhetoric isn't seeping into their heads, but the prospect of working minimum wage jobs and being a meaningless cog in the American capitalist system is bleak and unpleasant. And there is no excuse for one of the richest nations in the free world to have a sub-par educational system.

I pity teachers coming up and honestly putting forth their all to be good at what they do. It really is a constant battle. I didn't realize it when I was growing up and going through the grades, but I do now, having stood behind the desk myself. I don't blame those that left. I was told that in North Carolina, there are thousands of vacancies every year, and though the state's education programs creates somewhere around 3,300 teachers annually, with only 1,800 of them taking jobs in the state. It doesn't take complex math to figure out that this leaves substantial vacancies. They've been trying to get teachers from out of state, from foreign countries, and may hire people who have four-year degrees and no teaching license, allowing them "up to three years to earn one" (these statistics are from the North Carolina Business Committee for Education). What's the cause of North Carolina's shortage of teachers? In an article by Steve Hartsoe of the AP, they are: rowdy classrooms, behavior problems and language barriers. I can attest to the latter as being difficult: Hispanic students, in particular, tend to think it's "funny" if they pretend not to know or understand English, and the days in which I covered English as a Second Language class, made my life difficult by rolling their shoulders when I tried to tell them to sit down, responded in Spanish ("¿Que?") or just ignored me. I don't buy the argument that these minority students act out because they're "bored" with their "inexperienced" teachers, when in the local District, there are plenty of teachers who are bilingual. I am not convinced that the Hispanic students that tug at my shirt and shout "Mister, Mister" again while following me around the room and not listening behave like that because it's a "cultural difference." It's Mom and Dad letting them have their way in *America*, where *America* stands for "act however you want!"

I also don't buy the insistence that teaching is an honorable profession. It may have been, decades ago. But it's almost as if being educated, these days, isn't stressed nearly enough. It became apparent - to myself, at least - that by continuing to go in, whenever I was called by one of the sub callers, to teach, I was wasting my time and theirs. When asked whether I was looking for a full-time teaching job, I would hem and haw and give different answers to everyone (I busy myself with other things and often wonder how I find the time to get proper rest). Having seen how it's really run - I test drove the car before I got my driver's license - I couldn't see myself continuing on, and wanted to act as a giant warning flag to those that might be curious. I was a $90-a-day whore, a babysitter/cop, witnessing the system in its mixed-up glory, dealing with children who could care less in a country that's obsessed with its own children and the *idea* of education, but gets hazy when it comes to actually correcting the system so it runs properly, and restoring some dignity to the profession. Before that happens, it will be more of the same: stolen computers, school shootings, endless testing, belligerent behavior, low test scores, parents acting like their kids and not being parents, teachers under great stress, poor decision making, high turnover rate and the unavoidable Fear of Children.

To everyone: what happened?

50955114R00074

Made in the USA
Columbia, SC
12 February 2019